IMAGES
*of America*

# THE OHIO STATE
# UNIVERSITY NEIGHBORHOODS

**SPEEDY DELIVERY, C. 1926.** The Ohio State University and the surrounding neighborhoods' close ties with the university are reflected in this image of Poonah Baker, seated on her bicycle, in front of Brown Hall. Baker, a lifelong resident of the area, born in the Beers/Baker log cabin, carried the Ohio State *Lantern* on a regular route. Each of the elements in the image is now gone: Poonah Baker Gibney died in 1998, *Lantern* delivery vanished long ago, and Brown Hall fell to the wrecking ball in 2009. (George Zeigler and the family of Conn Baker.)

*On the cover:* Hennicks on North High Street, next to Long's Bookstore, was a popular spot for Ohio State students and residents in the 1940s. (The Ohio State University Archives.)

IMAGES
*of* America

# THE OHIO STATE UNIVERSITY NEIGHBORHOODS

Doreen N. Uhas Sauer and Stuart J. Koblentz
on behalf of the University District Organization

ARCADIA
PUBLISHING

Published by Arcadia Publishing
Charleston, South Carolina


Library of Congress Control Number: 2009920481

For all general information contact Arcadia Publishing at:
Telephone 843-853-2070
Fax 843-853-0044
E-mail sales@arcadiapublishing.com
For customer service and orders:
Toll-Free 1-888-313-2665

Visit us on the Internet at www.arcadiapublishing.com

# CONTENTS

# ACKNOWLEDGMENTS

Books such as this are the result of many people and organizations coming together and pooling resources, images, facts, memories, and leads.

We would like to thank the following community members for stepping forward and sharing their images of university area neighborhoods: Steve Abbott; Dick and Sandra Allen; Bill Brownson; Marty Davis Cottrill; Linda Snashall Cummins; Ed and Dianne Efsic; Emily Foster; Jerry Gordon; Curtis and Charmagne Hough; Joyce Hughes; Oliver, Matthew, and Nora Jones; the Marshall family; Cynthia Pavey Reith; Harold E. Rowe; Bill and Mary Riley; Jonathan Riley; William P. Rutherford; Nick Taggert; David J. Weltner; George Zeigler; the family of Conn Baker Gibney; Joe Motil; Judy Spencer Cohen; Sally Poston Bertolazzi; Roger Gibson and family; and Steve Heise.

The Ohio State University Archives, First Unitarian Universalist Church of Columbus, the Ohio Historical Society, University Baptist Church, University Community Organization, Campus Partners, and the University District Organization also provided images from their files and archives.

Others who helped our efforts while we were hunting, gathering, and writing include Joe Blundo and the *Columbus Dispatch*, Teresa Carstenen, Duryea Kemp, Kevlin Haire, Ed Lentz and the Bill Arter family, and the staff and board of the University District Organization: Ellen Moore, Pasquale Grado, Steve Sterrett, Susan Jennings, Bill Graver, Sharon Young, Patrick Harsch, and especially Richard Hollingsworth, student affairs of The Ohio State University. Stuart J. Koblentz would especially like to thank Jason Jones and Danny Stout. We would also like to recognize Arcadia Publishing and our editor, Melissa Basilone, for their faith in our project and their expertise in helping this become a reality.

Finally, we would each like to recognize our partners in life John Sauer and E Haley for helping us and believing in our project.

# INTRODUCTION

There will be no standard local history statements of who founded the township or what the Methodists did for the community (though I am sure it was great); local history sometimes needs a personal essay.

When I came to Columbus in 1965, transferring from another university, I was hungry for a city. The gap between Cleveland and Bowling Green had been too large. In Bowling Green, at the time, schoolchildren were bused to a railroad overpass to understand the concept of "hill." They "oooed" and "awweed." I left Bowling Green, Ohio, for Columbus. There was no turning back to Cleveland; I was officially part of the Cleveland diaspora.

As luck would have it, my Columbus apartment overlooked the Beers log cabin on East Norwich Avenue, my friend lived in a turreted mansion on East Fourteenth Avenue, and when I was bored, I could take a bus downtown, closely studying the 19th-century derelict High Street buildings. There were few places in the university neighborhoods I did not explore on foot, and when I began teaching, I taught at the first junior high in the nation, next door to a quirky old building that in 1904 had been the bathhouse for the Indianola Park pool, the largest in Ohio.

I could not escape the immediacy of nearby history. I do not remember such intimate places in Cleveland where one could touch history in the same way. Beautiful buildings, yes, but the Federal Reserve building in Cleveland did not move me. David Beers's log cabin did. In the late 1960s, my students arrived at school integrated but left in segregated little groups heading home. There were some rich students but more who were poor. White students headed north for home; black students headed south. They often saw the neglected but once lovely old homes in the neighborhood as embarrassing and "ghetto." On warm days, my classes left school, books in hand. I devised lessons that could be done on front walks and steps.

We studied proper nouns at the Neil Mansion within a lesson about the Underground Railroad and commas near Mirror Lake, where I sensed (these were different times) my students were not welcome. They told me they had never crossed High Street before. Once, at the Beers cabin, Poonah invited us into the dark and spacious interior. There was no setting more magical. Backyard History, as a course, was launched with a small grant. We put the school on the National Register of Historic Places. A parent anonymously donated the bronze plaque. When we opened the package, we might as well have been Joseph Smith with the gold tablets.

Years later, when Indianola Junior High was threatened with closure, an editorial appeared in the Ohio State University *Lantern*, the student paper, speaking out against the closure. The editor argued against the closing because the historic school was embedded in a community rich in history. The sacred spaces of the library with a wood-burning fireplace and the peaked attic that held old school maps and the boiler room where a child disappeared in 1933—would all be gone. How could one learn? The editor felt history needed to surround the history books. (The 20-something *Lantern* editor had been my 12-year-old student.)

I understood then how "nearby history" was the small door. Essayist Wendell Berry has said, "Real community is neighborhood; all else is metaphor."

—Doreen N. Uhas Sauer

# One

# NORTH COLUMBUS

It may be obvious that, between the earliest part of the 19th century and the 1870s, the neighborhoods that surrounded the university evolved from farmland and grew into concrete. This seems like an opening to a religious tract that states out of chaos came order. In 1800, the neighborhoods were no vast plain of grasses. This was not Kansas. The high spots (as in High Street) were animal trails and Shawnee paths from hunting to fishing grounds. No one laid out Route 23; they only paved it. Slate Run (Glen Echo), Iuka Ravine, and the little remembered Neil Run Creek led to an Olentangy River that looked far different from the one that was reshaped by Ohio State University in the 1920s. Narrower and swampy, the river split in two places forming the North and South Islands. In 1812, during the New Madrid earthquake, the Olentangy had been pushed out of its original bed. The neighborhood has a strong water theme. Had it not been for the sweet water of Mirror Lake (William Neil's spring), would there have been a sale that placed Ohio State University where it did?

Out of chaos, order may or may not come. But in Clinton Township and Columbus, out of chaos, platted boundaries and lots for sale would come. It is a developer's town. A second strong theme, after water, is speculation. Land in Ohio was relatively cheap for poor Welsh tenants and native-born Virginians, Pennsylvanians, and Kentuckians. With a separate town, North Columbus (1842), having already been established before the start of the Ohio Agricultural and Mechanical College (1871), the neighborhoods will not fill in smoothly from south to north. They will fill in by "following the money" from streetcar lines and road improvement contracts to huge land tracts, which will eventually all be sold by only a few families, mostly Neils. And by the end of the Civil War, Columbusites are well positioned to reap the rewards of having been on the winning side. Education, cleverness, and business acumen will grow neighborhoods. It will be relatively easy for North Columbus businessmen to gather $100,000 investments for a sewer pipe factory. Perhaps that is why David Beers's simple story is so compelling. Before 1870, there are many such stories.

**CABIN WITH A STORY.** David Beers Sr. (born 1746) built this log cabin at High Street near Dodridge Avenue after bringing his family from northeastern Pennsylvania to Ohio. At seven, David, his mother, and his young sister were taken by Native Americans and were separated. David was released and decades later found his sister, who had married a Wyandot chief. David, his wife Elizabeth, and their nine children made the cabin their home beginning in 1804. Beers lived to be 104; the cabin is still standing. (Doreen N. Uhas Sauer.)

**THE DEALER.** William Neil purchased the Vance farm in the 1820s, and it became the new Ohio Agricultural and Mechanical College 50 years later. His connection to the university neighborhoods is obvious; he once owned most of them from the Olentangy River to the state fairgrounds, downtown to Lane Avenue. His sons and daughters made their mark on the neighborhoods as well—Robert and Henry Neil (Indianola Avenue), Anne Neil Dennison (Dennison Place), and Elizabeth J. Neil McMillan (NECKO and Circles neighborhood). (University District Organization.)

**RURAL UNIVERSITY NEIGHBORHOODS, C. 1870.** Joseph Guitner's 20-acre farm and residence were located on the northeast corner of Slate Run (Glen Echo) and the Worthington Plank Road (High Street) in 1872, north of the Beers log cabin. In later maps, Guitner's substantial house appears as the Clinton Grove Hotel. The stream, now enclosed, runs under High Street to the river. (University District Organization.)

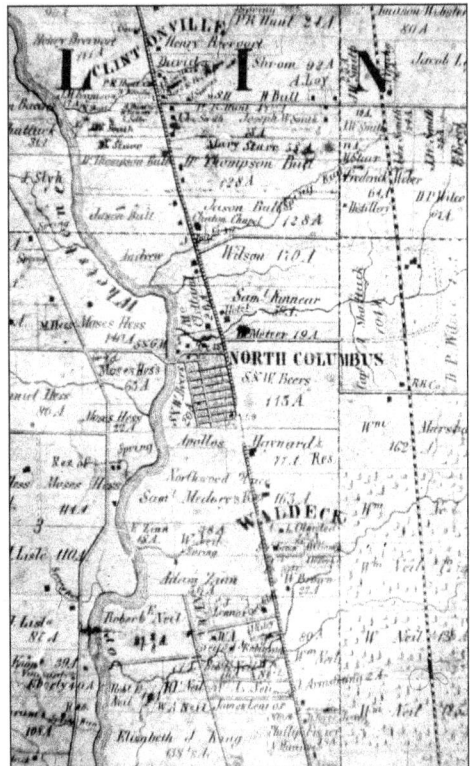

**THRIVING NORTH COLUMBUS.** Officially registered in 1852 by two of David Beers's sons, Solomon and George Washington Beers, North Columbus was platted smaller than the original area set aside in 1842 (to Woodruff Avenue). In 1852, Clintonville was "an accommodation" of houses for workers, and Waldeck became only an avenue. Two mansions can be discerned: the Apollo Maynard and the G. Williams (later Samuel Medary) residences. (University District Organization.)

**THE IRISH SURVEYOR FAMILY.**
Immigrant Samuel Kinnear came
to North Columbus in 1833,
opened a hotel, most likely the
Clinton Grove Hotel, and lived
at Tompkins and High Streets.
His second son, Josiah, a farmer
and surveyor, laid out North
Columbus with his father, hence
Kinnear Place and Kinnear Alley.
Samuel's wife was a Shattuck, a
name associated with the Glen
Echo neighborhood. (John Gray.)

**NO EAST–WEST ROAD.** There was no way across the Olentagy River until the 1870s, when a covered bridge was built at West Dodridge Street. William Neil and North Columbus businessmen ruled north–south road construction, building High Street in clay ($700 per mile) in 1834 (and again in 1849 and 1852). Even if the road turned to mud, a toll was collected. The company's charter was revoked; wrathful citizens tore down the Olentangy Street tollgates. (Marty Davis Cottrill.)

**NORTH AND DODRIDGE STREETS.** Looking north from a muddy Dodridge Street, the Beers mill in the picture would eventually be joined by additional mills and distilleries. Rosewell Wilcox's sawmill, built adjacent to the Beers gristmill on the same flume, caused some family litigation. (Wilcox's son was married to a Beers daughter.) The Brown residence, Welsh millers who married into the Beers family, sits on the hill to the right. (Judy Spencer Cohen.)

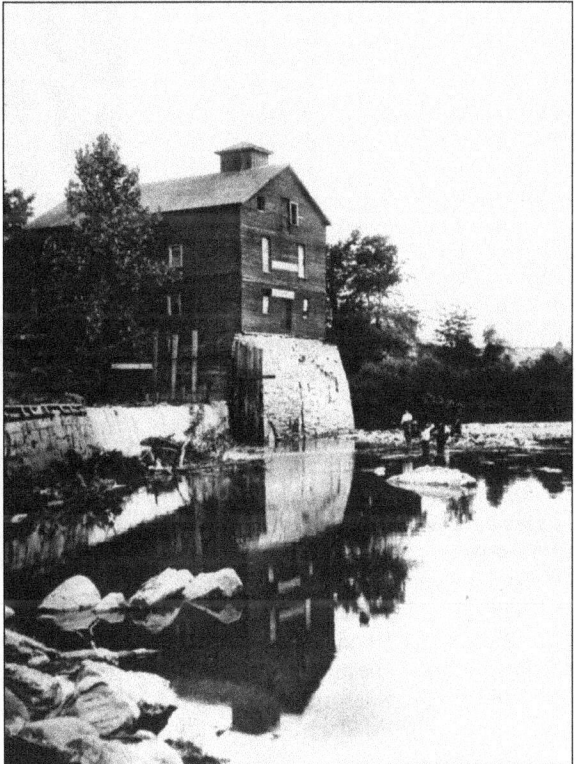

**FIRST FRANKLIN COUNTY GRISTMILL.** In 1810, David Beers's mill saved settlers a trip to Chillicothe, and Beers's ability to speak Native American languages helped establish the mill as a trading post. The mill eventually passed to John Piatt, father of James Piatt, the poet and builder of the Piatt Castle in Champaign County, and then to the Hess family. Through much of the 20th century, the pioneer mills and foundations, on the edge of Olentangy Park, were places to play. (Marty Davis Cottrill.)

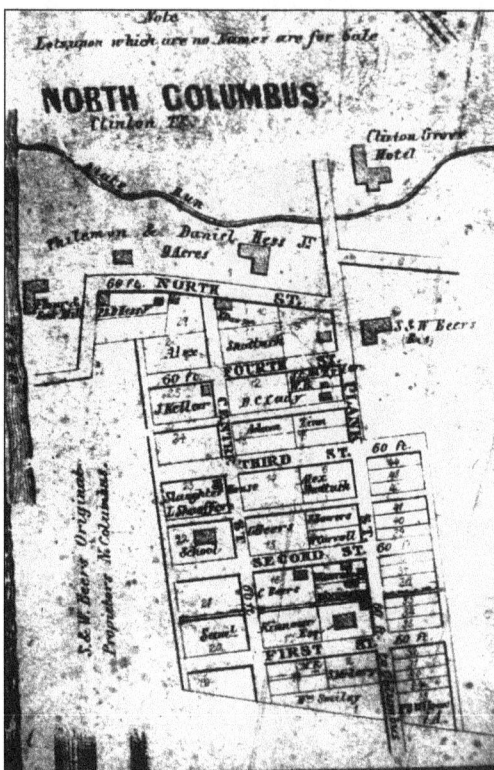

**SLAUGHTER HOUSE WITH NEARBY SCHOOL, 1856.** A transportation node for stagecoaches travelling between Columbus and Sandusky (now Route 23), North Columbus grew, and in 1871, it was annexed to Columbus. First through Fourth Streets and Front Street would become Tompkins, Hudson, Duncan, Dodridge Streets, and Neil Avenue, respectively, to avoid confusion with streets downtown. Columbus Public Schools bought the 20-seat schoolhouse for $3,620, indicating respectable property values, even if next to a slaughter house. (University District Organization.)

**FAMOUS CONFEDERATE SYMPATHIZER.** Samuel Medary, an outspoken Copperhead journalist, in an era filled with abolitionist and equally outspoken citizens, outraged Columbus Lincoln supporters as editor of the *Ohio Statesman*. Medary died shortly after his newspaper office was burned. His 28-room mansion, North Wood, on 162 acres became the Columbus Catholic College (1883–1887). By 1910, Medary's property became Northwood and Oakland Avenues, the back lane to his house became Medary Avenue. (The Ohio Historical Society.)

**SOCIAL CENTER OF THE RICH AND FAMOUS.** In 1856, Robert Neil built his mansion on a Native American mound overlooking what would become Fifteenth and Indianola Avenues. Robert married Lucas Sullivant's granddaughter, and his sister, Anne, married Ohio governor William Dennison. The house was visited by the famous and the discreet—a Bonaparte of France and escaping slaves. Robert's brother, Henry, inherited the house in 1870. The Kappa Sigma fraternity has owned it since 1908, remodeling it in 1938. (University District Organization.)

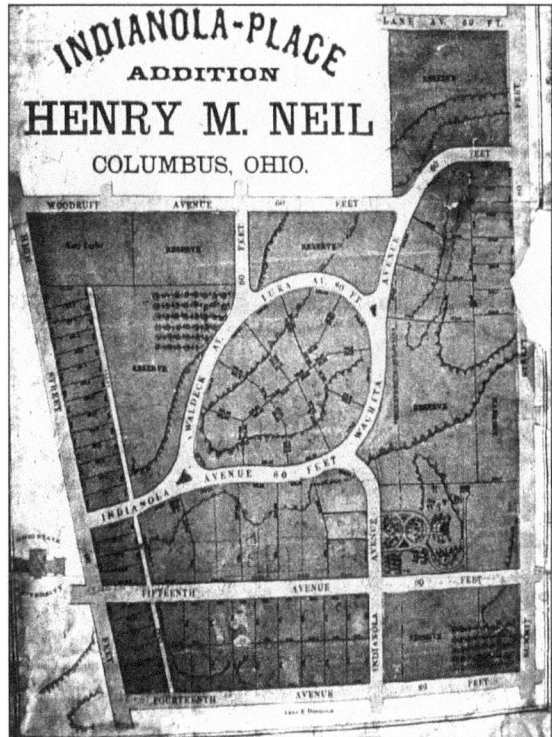

**AN INSPIRATION FOR NAMING.** Henry Neil gave the neighborhood a much copied name—*Indianola*. The first Ohioan to enlist in the Civil War for the Union, Neil was wounded at the Battle of Iuka, near Indianola, Mississippi. His house became Indianola and the curved carriage path, Iuka. The word *Indianola* has been attached to Indianola Forest Historic District, two schools, a major street, and numerous churches and businesses. Iuka is a boulevard park, winding through the Iuka Historic District. (University District Organization.)

15

**A UNION CAMP IN THE NEIGHBORHOOD.** The commissary of Camp Thomas (easily distinguished by white vertical siding) lasted until the 1960s at Wilcox Avenue and Dodridge Street. Camp Thomas, established on the Solonion Beers farm in 1861, included 120 Union men, formerly prisoners of war in Mumfordsville, Kentucky. Gen. Lew Wallace (author of *Ben Hur*), a commander of the camp, was to make them combat-ready again. He complained that they disappeared from the camp, apparently not too keen on going back to the front lines. (Doreen N. Uhas Sauer.)

**THE LAST ORIGINAL.** The little one-room, one-story barbershop (17 West Dodridge Avenue) was reportedly the last pre–Civil War store in North Columbus. It was moved around the corner from its original location on North High Street (between Catherine Ramlow and Son's Dry Goods at 2661 North High Street and Dr. Gratthouse's office at 2651 North High Street) to accommodate the building of the second-generation Italianate commercial buildings. The barbershop was torn down in the 1990s. (Joe Motil.)

16

# *Two*

# THE LAND GRANT COLLEGE

The push for the creation of an agricultural college first began with the Ohio Board of Agriculture and the Ohio State Grange. With the enactment of the Morrill Act and Pres. Abraham Lincoln's signature, the idea of farmers' education was born. As a land-grant college, Ohio State University felt the responsibility to influence the welfare of people in education, agriculture, and industrial growth. An institution of higher learning with a civic, social, and even moral responsibility is an ideal situation for collaborations between a bureaucracy and small centers of civic-mindedness. Between 1870 and 1900, the signs were very positive.

Ohio State University president James Canfield created High School Day, opening up the university in May 1897 to thousands of visitors to explore higher education. Morning trains brought in huge numbers of high school students. Arrangements for a hillside lunch near the spring had to be pulled inside because of the weather, but the day was considered a success. His own daughter Dorothy was an extraordinary reformer and outspoken advocate for her causes. She is one symbol of the environment that nurtured her—educated and tough.

There are few defined neighborhoods, but there are neighborhood people. Italians and African Americans will form one small neighborhood, the Welsh, newly arrived, will add to North Columbus. The neighborhoods to the south of the university will begin to fill in between downtown Columbus and Tenth Avenue, following the streetcar routes of North High Street and Neil Avenue. Adjacent to the college are woods filled with violets (West Frambes Avenue) and Victorian mansions to the east and south. Young people, especially, from across Ohio, begin to settle in to the area.

**A FORGOTTEN NEIGHBORHOOD.** Italian and African American workers, among others, worked as stonemasons and brick layers to build University Hall and Ohio State University. Italians and African Americans, however, were often discriminated against in housing, and many families formed their own neighborhood at the end of West Lane to West Frambes Avenues. The houses lasted until shortly after the building of Ohio Stadium and the relocation of the Olentangy River. (The Ohio State University Archives.)

**MIRROR LAKE GIVES BIRTH TO COLLEGE, 1871.** After looking at many sites for the new Ohio Agricultural and Mechanical College, the trustees finalized their decision to buy William Neil's 331.11 acres for $117,508, after drinking from Neil's spring. A German trustee, after taking refreshing sips, stated, "It's hard to get a Dutchman away from a spring like that." In 1891, while installing a trunk sewer line through campus, the city struck the source of the spring, and in a day or two, it was completely dry—and has remained so for over 100 years. (The Ohio State University Archives.)

**BELOVED FIRST PRESIDENT, 1896.** Edward Orton Sr., also a professor of geology, is commemorated by a piece of the neighborhood. Orton Hall (1893), a building made of 40 different Ohio stones, was built to honor Orton, but his son, Dr. Edward Orton Jr., also wanted an immense glacial erratic boulder from Iuka Ravine. According to folklore, the boulder, found near North Fourth Street, originally coming by glacier from the Canadian Precambrian Shield 998 million years earlier, was rolled and dragged by students who loved Dr. Orton Sr. (The Ohio State University Archives.)

**STREETCAR LINES CHANGE PHILLIP FISHER'S GARDEN.** The installation of streetcar lines northward brought rapid commercialization. Two houses at Ninth Avenue and High Street illustrate this. In 1872, Phillip Fisher's garden was at the city's far north end. Three years later, the Domoney family houses were built. One house (right) was replaced with Albert Domoney's business (1926). The larger house, owned by Mr. Domoney's mother, became a men's rooming house, where Prof. Stillman W. Robinson (Ohio State's Robinson Laboratory) lived. The Domoney family owned the properties for over a century. (University District Organization.)

**DELIVERY WAGONS SERVE RESIDENTS.** North Columbus's self-contained and vibrant community had many businesses with interlocking economic and social ties among the families. The Henry Bower family, dry goods (2643 North High Street), with their large delivery wagons, was related to the John Bower Hardware Company (2602–2610 North High). Owners of Nigh Brothers' grocery, across the street, like the Bowers, sat on bank, undertaking, and church boards. (University District Organization.)

**THE CHEMICAL FIRE STATION, C. 1892.** Rapid growth of the neighborhoods from Fifteenth to Arcadia Avenues necessitated city fire, water, and sewer services. The firehouse, located at 2465 North High Street, opened in 1892 as station No. 2. In 1898, it was changed to station No. 13, and its successor and current firehouse No. 13, was built at Arcadia and Deming Avenues, when the Chemical Fire Station building was torn down in 1957. (Circulating Visuals, Columbus Metropolitan Library.)

**WORKERS AT LANDMARK BUSINESS C. 1880.** The Sewer Pipe Company opened on March 7, 1869, (present site of North High School) because a particular type of clay and soapstone shale was found in the Slate Run (Glen Echo) ravine. Equal in quality to the celebrated Middlebury stone of England, which up until this time had produced the finest sewer pipe in the world, the discovery prompted North Columbus businessmen to hire a supervisor from England, build two kilns, and make the company a major north end employer. (Judy Spencer Cohen.)

**AN OUTING WITH THE MATRIARCH.** Catherine Ramlow (center, dark bonnet) is seated with sister, Elizabeth (right, dark dress), and family, probably at Hayden Run Falls in the early 1890s. A successful businesswoman, Catherine came from Germany in the 1850s. Formidable and hardworking, she and her husband worked at the American House Hotel, accumulating enough to start their own business. As a widow, Catherine and her son, Peter, created the Northern Savings Bank and eventually built the Ramlow Block, the most prominent building of North Columbus. (John Gray.)

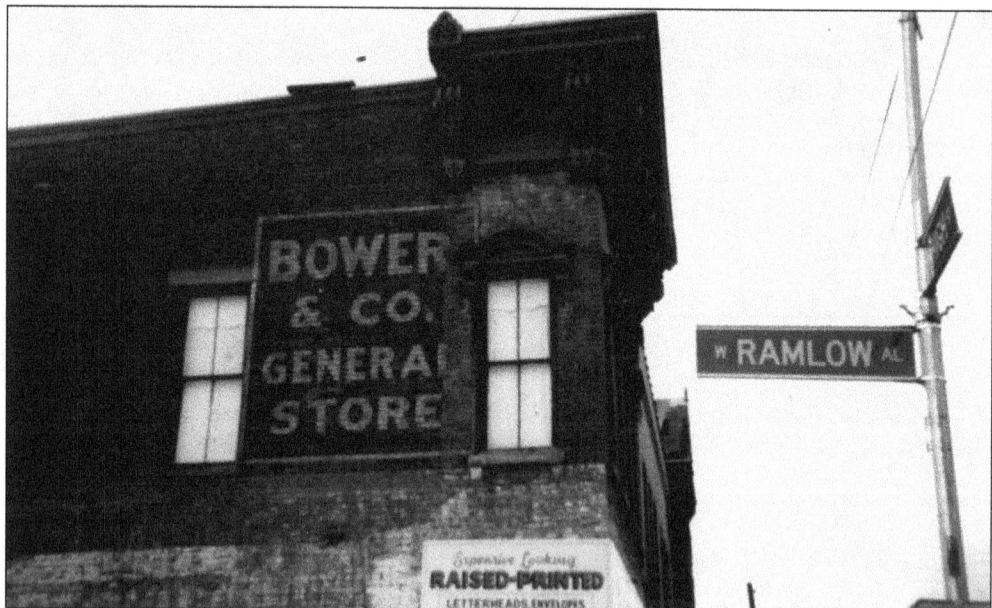

**"GHOST SIGNS" OF SUCCESS.** Peter Ramlow did well. He changed the family name from Volker to Ramlow for business reasons, married into the wealthy Hess family, and saw his descendants, the Straits, marry into the Casto family (shopping center developers). As a child, Peter's great-grandson would remember sitting on "his" block waiting for parents to shop or, later in the evening, watching outdoor movies projected on the side of the store. (John Gray.)

A QUIET MOMENT FOR REMEMBERING. Eliza Beers Brown sits in the side yard of 101 West Maynard Avenue, the home of her daughter and son-in-law, Martha (Brown) and Edward Grove. Born in 1846, Eliza had grown up in North Columbus, in a house near Duncan Avenue and High Street, on her father Solomon's farm. Eliza married William Brown, who came as a boy from Llanidloes, Wales. At one time, the mill built by David Beers, Eliza's grandfather, was run by Richard Brown, Eliza's father-in-law. (Marty Davis Cottrill.)

AT 1900 EAST NORWICH AVENUE. The drive to the Peasley farmhouse (on the right) will become East Norwich Avenue. By positioning the cabin to the rear of the property, Conn Baker could watch cows pass the kitchen window to graze by the river. Baker's decision ensured that Norwich Avenue would have very deep lots, making the street attractive for apartment development by the 1970s. The house on the left would be replaced with St. Luke's Lutheran Church in 1923 (now St. Clare's Chapel), designed by famed architect Richard Reeves. (George Zeigler and the family of Conn Baker.)

**WELL-TO-DO MOVE TO NEIL AVENUE.** The John C. Sherwood home was designed by J. A. Jones, architect. Up-and-coming businessmen and the already wealthy lived in Victorian sumptuousness south of Ohio State University. The pressed brick with black mortar, brownstone trim, and curved plate glass windows at 1281 Neil Avenue are a testimony to the wealth of Sherwood, president of the Sherwood-Crippin Rubber (tires) Company and vice president of the Columbus Cement Stone Company. (Circulating Visuals, Columbus Metropolitan Library.)

**PRESTIGIOUS NEIGHBORHOOD.** The Elizabeth J. (Neil) McMillen Homestead Addition contains a variety of homes in NECKO (Neil, Eighth, Cannon, King Organization) neighborhood from around the 1890s. The home at 320 King Avenue belonged to Percival Yoerger, owner of the highly regarded Yoerger (electric and painted) Sign Company. The neighborhood acquired a reputation as home to Ohio State professors. Four of them were prominent enough to have a campus building named in their honor—Embury Hitchcock, William Lazenby, Nathanial Lord, Alfred Vivian. (Steve and Martha Hewitt.)

**MEMORIAL DAY, C. 1888.** Aided by the streetcar lines stretching northward, neighborhoods grew along North Fourth Street. From Fifth to Chittenden Avenues, attached row houses in courtyard settings (streetcar suburbs) provided housing for young families (now New Indianola Historic District in Weinland Park). From Fifteenth through Eighteenth Avenues, large homes were built for professionals like Dr. David Summy, 1831 North Fourth Street, who was superintendent and chief surgeon for the Hartman Sanitarium. (Doreen N. Uhas Sauer.)

**A LONE SECOND EMPIRE HOUSE.** William A. Sharp, a well-known Columbus attorney, had his home at 82 Sixteenth Avenue designed by noted architect Herbert Linthwaite. The house sat on acreage purchased from the Robert Neil estate. Sixteenth and Seventeenth Avenues from Indianola Avenue to Summit Street were dominated by large and even ostentatious mansions, most of which were demolished in the 1970s for apartments. However, this one remains, greatly altered (see page 86). (Circulating Visuals, Columbus Metropolitan Library.)

**SISTERS WITH A PIONEER PAST.**
Bess (Grove) Tudor and her sister
Ruth (Grove) Rutherford grew up
only blocks away from where their
great-great-grandfather David Beers had
built a log cabin in 1804. Ruth, who
married Perry E. Rutherford and lived
her entire life in the neighborhood,
wrote a small book on the history of
the area, which is still an invaluable
resource. (Marty Davis Cottrill.)

**THE WHAT TO DO CLUB, 1890s.** A group of eighth-grade girls at Northwood School organized a club for self-improvement and to stay in touch after eighth grade, the final year of formal education. The girls' club was probably named for a then-popular Pansy Series of books, The What to Do Girls. One girl would read aloud as others did "fancy work." Decades later, the girls continued to gather regularly from 1909 until 1952, when only three living members remained: Marian Grimm, Nellie Hicks, and Martha Brown Grove (sitting center in front). (Marty Davis Cottrill.)

**ONE OF 10 MOST IMPORTANT WOMEN.** Dorothy (Canfield) Fisher, second row, left, pictured around 1898 with her Kappa Kappa Gamma sisters, was university president James Canfield's daughter, who went from the neighborhood to much more. She spoke five languages, wrote 40 books, supported women's rights and racial equality, and was a personal friend of First Lady Eleanor Roosevelt, who named her one of America's 10 most important women in the 1930s. Dorothy brought the Montessori method of child development to the United States. She also created the country's first adult education program and shaped the nation's reading tastes by helping select book-of-the-month club selections from 1925 to 1951. Another neighborhood resident and influential historian, Arthur Schlesinger Jr. lived at 1806 North High Street in the Fairfax Apartments as a child, while his father, Arthur Schlesinger Sr., taught history at Ohio State. (The Ohio State University Archives.)

**NORTHWOOD SCHOOL, 1890s.** Northwood School (2231 North High Street) had more than 800 students housed in 27 rooms. Built in 1879 with an addition in 1905, the school was a significant part of life in the university neighborhoods. It closed after a bitter battle of neighbors against the Columbus Public Schools in the 1970s. The Columbus schools said the loss of families in the area meant fewer children; the neighbors asserted that closing the school would lead to fewer families and children. (Doreen N. Uhas Sauer.)

**NORTHWOOD CLASS, C. 1890.** The proliferation of elementary public schools built within 20 years shows the neighborhoods' rapid growth. These children lived between Blake and Woodruff Avenues and between the river and Indianola Avenue. Other elementary schools included: Eighth Avenue School (1889, addition 1905), Indianola School (1907), Medary School (1892), Ninth Avenue School (1896), and Fifth Avenue School (1886). The only high school was the (old) North High at Fourth and Dennison Avenues. (University District Organization.)

VICTORIAN ARCHITECTURE PROMPTS CRITICISM. Fifth Avenue School (Fifth and Highland Avenues) today is a highly successful alternative school with an international focus in a school designed without walls. The original school (seen here) was built in 1886. Sixteen rooms housed more than 500 elementary students who resided in approximately 16 blocks. Public outcry criticized the board of education for spending money on schools with towers and gingerbread. Though demolished, the building's original steps and stone posts are on the playground in front of the new school. (Circulating Visuals, Columbus Metropolitan Library.)

THE WHITE CHURCH. By 1893, Welsh immigrants and new electric streetcars pushed the need for larger churches for Congregationalists. North Congregationalist Church (55 East Blake Avenue), nicknamed the White Church, incorporated the original Welsh Congregational Church across the street (sold to be a rug weaving factory). The area's emigration had a direct connection to Montgomeryshire, Wales, where ministers fed unrest among the poor Welsh tenant farmers, urging them to move to the United States. (Judy Spencer Cohen.)

**RESPECTABILITY AND CULTURE.** By the late 1890s, skilled labor and business owners lived north of the university, and industrial titans and professional classes lived south. Settlement patterns followed streetcar lines. A rising middle class, who had more leisure time than their grandparents, formed reading circles, such as the Northwood Literary and the Eleventh Avenue Reading Clubs. A house filled with popular bric-a-brac also gave an air of culture. (University District Organization.)

**QUIET BEFORE THE STORM.** In 1897, West Frambes Avenue seemed residential but pastoral, even though Granville Frambes, a Union Civil War hero, had sold his large farm to the fledgling college across the street a few years earlier. To the right of the picture (now St. Stephen's Episcopal Church), young couples strolled in the woods known for an abundance of violets. To the left (now Ramseyer Hall), the iron fences marked the yards of working-class families. Peasley Avenue, named for the family on Norwich Avenue, became Curl Drive. (University District Organization.)

# *Three*

# THE AMAZING CONN BAKER

Artist Conn Baker was a man of amazing accomplishments, yet some 60 years after his death, few know of his daring, his artistic talent, or the log cabin that he saved and made his home. For five decades, from the 1890s through the 1940s, his concern for the cabin made it that such a wonderful treasure for the University District would remain intact. The eldest son of Burr and Jenny Baker, he was born in Toledo in 1871, and he later moved with his family to Columbus when he was a youngster. By his teens, Baker developed superior athletic skills and focused his attention on bicycle racing, a sport in its infancy. After conquering that field and holding numerous speed records, he melded sport with a love of daring deeds and created Diavolo, a circus act that propelled him to the pinnacle of the Forepaugh Sells Circus, besting Ringling Brothers Circus in excitement.

In 1899, Conn Baker and his brother Herman Baker purchased the David Beers cabin, moving it from North Columbus to East Norwich Avenue. There it became an art studio for the brothers, both artists.

The two-story log structure, with its oak flooring, is capable of bearing enormous weight. Conn and Herman were known for bringing cows and other large animals into the cabin to serve as subjects for pastoral paintings. Parts of a second cabin were added to enlarge the building for a family home for Conn and his wife Laura. Daughter Poonah Baker Gibney and grandson Conn Baker Gibney also made the cabin their home in time. Because of the family's purchase and preservation of the Beers cabin, Columbus's oldest existing building can continue to be a jewel in the crown of the university neighborhoods, secure for generations to come.

**JENNY BAKER, RESIDENT, NORWICH AVENUE.** Built by the Peasley family, this 19th-century farmhouse was purchased by the Baker family after they relocated from Toledo to Columbus. Later a second-story porch was added. The barbed wire fence in the foreground was used to keep livestock from wandering off the premises and to keep horses from getting into the yard. (George Zeigler and the family of Conn Baker.)

**THE DAREDEVIL.** A champion bicyclist, Conn Baker was known as a daredevil in his youth. In 1894, while at Lookout Mountain, Tennessee, Baker held on tightly, dangling 1,800 feet aboveground. The picture stands as evidence of his superb athletic ability, as well as, his ability to accomplish what the faint of heart could not dare imagine. (George Zeigler and the family of Conn Baker.)

THE ONE, THE ONLY, DIAVOLO! Dressed in a red flock costume, complete with devil horns, Baker, as Diavolo, would scale the ladder to the top of a wooden ramp, mount his bicycle, and use his bicycle racing know-how (and sheer nerve) to plunge down the ramp, through a 360-degree loop, 37 feet in diameter, and emerge unscathed. Diavolo made his American debut on April 2, 1902, with the Forepaugh Sells Circus. While others before him had tried, all were either injured or killed while attempting the stunt, making Baker the first to cheat death. The act was an enormous success in the early 1900s, as it combined bicycling, speed, real danger, and showmanship. (Doreen N. Uhas Sauer.)

---

# DIAVOLO

J. C. CARTER.

◎

## Looping the Loop on a Bicycle.

EN ROUTE SEASON OF 1906, INDIA, CHINA & THE EAST INDIES
**WITH HARMSTON'S GRAND CIRCUS.**

| EASTERN ADDRESS, | PERMANENT HOME ADDRESS. |
|---|---|
| CARE H. A. ABRAMS, SINGAPORE S. S. | 44 E. NORWICH AVENUE, COLUMBUS, OHIO, U. S. A. |

---

DIAVOLO HANDBILL. Billed as the act that is "Veritable Ca-Sheaf of All Hazardous Exploits," J. C. Carter (Conn Baker's stage name) was Diavolo. While on tour in Asia, Baker's skills elicited excitement in people from all walks of life. Invitation scrolls, printed on silk, were extended to the wealthy and powerful so they could see the unimaginable. (George Zeigler and the family of Conn Baker.)

33

**CONN BAKER, C. 1904.** Following a successful athletic career as a competitive bicyclist and daredevil, Conn Baker began to make plans to settle down once he met Laura Calvert, who was also performing in Asia at the time. (George Zeigler and the family of Conn Baker.)

**LAURA CALVERT BAKER, C. 1904.** The love of Conn Baker's life, Laura Calvert was a native of Great Britain and a successful and popular musical comedienne as part of the Tiller Girls. The couple met in India, and they were married in Bedford, England. Laura Calvert Baker died in Columbus in 1965. (George Zeigler and the family of Conn Baker.)

**BEERS/BAKER CABIN IN NEW SETTING.** Originally built north of the corner of North High Street and Dodridge Street, the David Beers cabin had been unoccupied for years when Conn Baker purchased it. After dismantling it, Baker moved it to Norwich Avenue, adjacent to his family's home, along the path the cows took to the Olentangy River. What is notable about this 1904 image is the lack of any buildings north of the cabin. Northwood Avenue had yet to be built. (George Zeigler and the family of Conn Baker.)

**DARING YOUNG MEN AND THEIR MOTORCYCLES.** To modern eyes, the earliest motorcycles look like bicycles with engines attached to them—and that is essentially what they were in the early 1900s. It would stand to reason that Conn Baker, one-time bicycle-racing record holder and daredevil, would have an interest in the vehicle and the sport. (George Zeigler and the family of Conn Baker.)

# A GOOD PLACE TO GO

Dear Sir:-- ........................ Columbus, Ohio, September 10, 1915

A meeting of the Sixteenth Ward Republican Club will be held at Conn Baker's Log Cabin, September 13th, 1915, at eight o'clock.

This is the meeting for the annual election of officers, and your presence is earnestly requested. Come and bring a friend.

The Hon. E. L. Taylor will address the club.

W. E. BARNETT, Secretary

JAMES N. LINTON, President

**A GOOD PLACE TO GO, 1915.** A loyal Republican from the party of Lincoln and the days of Pres. Theodore Roosevelt, Conn Baker was actively involved in local party politics. This postcard, with Baker's sketch of his cabin, was mailed to the faithful for an election of local officers. Contemporary newspaper accounts of the meetings covered these happenings extensively. (George Zeigler and the family of Conn Baker.)

STORYTELLING TIME, C. 1910. One of Conn Baker's other art forms was the preservation of stories, pioneer tales, and oral histories of early Ohio from the time of David Beers, the cabin's builder. Taken in the cabin's main room (now the living room), this image shows the interior of the cabin. The chair and tree stump on which the subjects sit remain in the house today. However, the identity of the storyteller and young listener remain unknown. (George Zeigler and the family of Conn Baker.)

**QUIET MOMENTS DOING WHAT ONE LOVES.** The cabin and its grounds were subjects for many landscape paintings. Brothers Herman and Conn Baker took advantage of a warm spring afternoon to create their art together. After his death, Conn's work remained in the cabin, just as he had left it. (George Zeigler and the family of Conn Baker.)

**A MODEL SUBJECT.** The cabin's second floor was used as the Bakers' arts studio after skylights were added. An unidentified model poses for artists in the second floor studio of the cabin. The hats in the foreground belong to Herman and Conn Baker; however, the name of the artist in the photograph, and the model, are unknown. (George Zeigler and the family of Conn Baker.)

**PLEASED TO MEET YOU.** Master Kay Gibney greets his father, Kenneth, as mother, Miriam (Poonah) looks on. Miriam was affectionately known as Poonah, named for the city in India in which her parents were engaged. Taken in the cabin's front yard, looking southeast, the image shows the location of Poonah's childhood tree house, as well as the homes on East Norwich Avenue. (George Zeigler and the family of Conn Baker.)

**POONAH BAKER GIBNEY AND CHILDREN.** Conn and Laura Baker's daughter, Poonah, poses on the side doorsteps of the cabin in the 1930s. Seated with her are her sons, Conn Baker Gibney (left) and Kay J. Gibney. During her lifetime, Poonah, like her father, had great affection for the cabin, which she passed on to both her sons. Throughout her life, Poonah would invite classes of schoolchildren in to see the cabin. (George Zeigler and the family of Conn Baker.)

**LAURA AND CONN BAKER, C. 1930.** Conn and Laura Baker relax in the yard of their home on East Norwich Avenue on what appears to have been a warm summer afternoon. Conn is wearing plus fours, a knicker-styled pant. Laura's hose, rolled down, illustrate one way to keep cool on hot and humid days. (George Zeigler and the family of Conn Baker.)

**CONN BAKER AND HIS HIGH WHEEL, C. 1942.** Conn Baker, in vintage attire, sits astride a penny-farthing bicycle on Fifteenth Avenue near Sullivant Hall. Popular in the 1880s, the large wheel allowed greater distance with less effort; however, the bikes were dangerous. Riders easily toppled over in sudden stops. The bikes, called "the wheel," lost favor with the invention of the safety bicycle and the pneumatic bicycle tire in the 1890s. (George Zeigler and the family of Conn Baker.)

# Four

# NEIGHBORHOODS RISING

If there was a golden age for every city, every town, every neighborhood, it would seem that the first and second decade of the 20th century would be the university neighborhood's time. Both the neighborhoods and Ohio State University were relatively young. There was a superintendent of schools with strength and vision, an Ohio State University president who saw himself primarily as a progressive and a preacher, and a city mayor who remained largely distant from the university area.

There was expansion and social prominence. Newspapers were filled with flattering accounts of plans for magnificent new structures, like the new King Avenue Methodist Church, originally designed with two-story turrets on either side of the main doors, like the Castle in Buda. In 1908, the city council added large tracts of land from the Indianola Heights Addition and Indianola Park to land on either side of the Cleveland, Cincinnati, Chicago and St. Louis Railway, known as the Big Four Railroad. A magnificent hotel was planned for Fourteenth Avenue and North High Street with rooms for professors and students, private dining rooms for families and clubs, and electric light and hot-water heating throughout. The York Lodge was being built at Smith Place and High Street for an estimated $90,000, and after 40 years in service, the old North Dormitory on Neil Avenue was being torn down. Showman Al G. Field bought three large dwellings in Indianola Forest, and a house on Fourteenth Avenue was selling for $20,000 in 1908.

It was a golden age. Not because students and residents and university officials behaved with collaboration in mind but simply because all of them were relatively prosperous. The mayor had real problems in the rest of the city to deal with, but this part of the city had few blemishes. The only hint of imperfection peeks out with the educational partnership of community and university, which produced the junior high movement. The impetus is that most students were leaving school after eighth grade. In the downtown areas of the Badlands, hundreds of eighth-grade girls worked as prostitutes near Fort Hayes Barracks. There was no hint of this in the university neighborhoods, but using the junior high concept in an area where there was community and college support, the idea could be tested.

In the first decades of the 20th century, institutions and traditions would be established—the Pavey family; Hennicks restaurant; Thurbur's humorous stories; and the Indianola School. Other trademarks of the neighborhoods would start to vanish—North Columbus as a separate town; Ohio Field; and the garden rivalry between Oakland and Northwood Avenues.

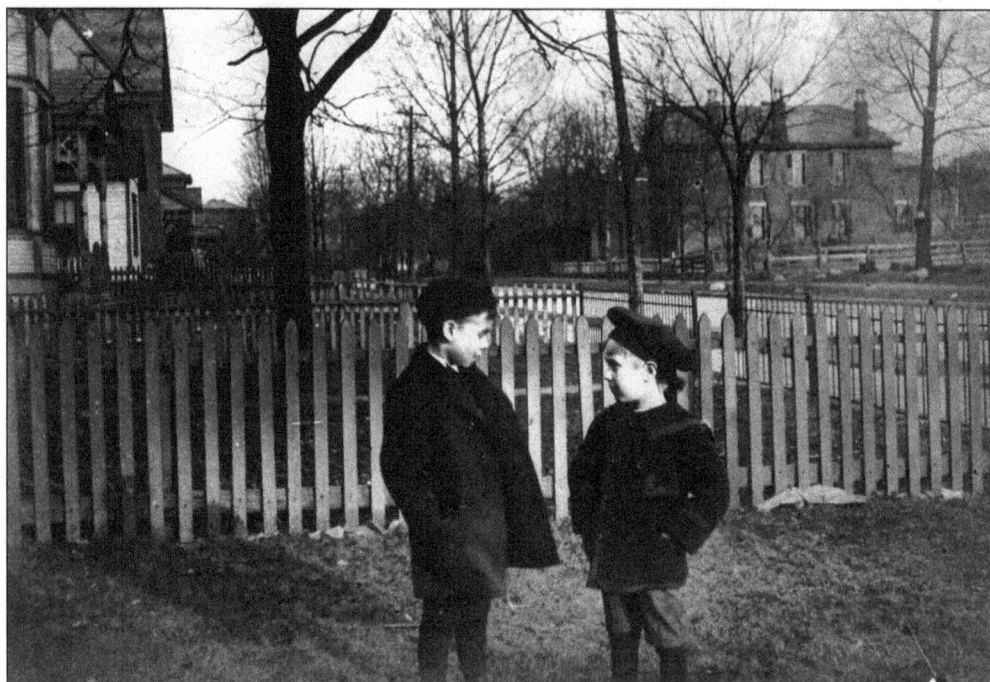

COUSINS ON NINTH AVENUE, C. 1900. Barton Griffith Jr. (right) and Harry Fox (left) stand in Griffith's yard at 68 West Ninth Avenue, looking east to High Street. On the right side, the Elliott house stands out with a new porch across the front. According to neighbors, "Mrs. Elliott was just so proud of that porch." On the left, beyond the white frame house, is the Streeper home (44 West Ninth Avenue), torn down in 1958 to make way for the first of the new apartment houses on the block. (University District Organization.)

OHIO FIELD, 1909. Neighborhood houses on High Street and West Woodruff Avenue (now gone) form the boundaries of Ohio (University) Field, built one year earlier. Houses on High Street still exist behind commercial buildings. This view, looking northeast, shows Medary School in the distance. Football fed the passions of Columbus, but with a seating capacity of only 6,100, Ohio Field had overflow crowds. The field was enlarged several times until capacity reached 14,000. (The Ohio State University Archives.)

**A CIVIC-MINDED NEIGHBOR, 1912.** Ohio State University president William Oxley Thompson (1899–1925) was an accomplished equestrian and a national leader in World War I. He saw himself as a Presbyterian minister first. In the neighborhood, he preached at a local church and baptized the children of Ohio State students. He helped to create the first junior high in the nation. He was larger than life in many ways, so it is fitting that his 14-foot statue has presided over the oval since 1930. (The Ohio State University Archives.)

**A BREAK FROM STUDYING.** Fraternities and sororities generally did not have houses in the early years of the university. If they were lucky, they rented, but often only year to year, and rarely at the same spot. The Sigma Pi fraternity was much more fortunate. Established at Ohio State University in 1903, the group maintained a prominent mansion at 244 West Tenth Avenue. (The Ohio State University Archives.)

**A STUDENT ROOM.** Ohio Agricultural and Mechanical College (and later Ohio State) students have boarded or found rooms within the university neighborhoods since before the beginning of the 20th century, and the basics of the rooms have not changed much over the decades— family photographs, piles of books (positioned to appear being used), posters advertising college activities, eclectic decorating with found items, and an alarm clock close by for early classes. (University District Organization.)

44

**THE GATE TO CAMPUS AND NEIGHBORHOOD, 1914.** Fraternity races begin near the intersection of Fifteenth Avenue and High Street. Before World War I, Fifteenth Avenue had not yet officially (or unofficially) been established as Greek Row. Yet student activities and high jinks popularly happened at the main entrance to Ohio State. The northeast corner of the intersection, seen in the background, is still there, although altered, and houses a coffee shop, a book exchange, and restaurants. (The Ohio State University Archives.)

**GREATEST 20TH-CENTURY AMERICAN HUMORIST.** James Thurber, neighborhood resident (sort of), was a "townie," living at home (77 Jefferson Avenue). After he dropped out of classes, he continued to take the streetcar each day to campus. His life (with or without classes) centered on the Phi Kappa Psi house and collaborations with fraternity brother Elliott Nugent. Their hit Broadway play, *The Male Animal*, a not-very-disguised satire of Columbus's football mania, debuted in its movie version on March 12, 1942, at the RKO Palace with much "officialdom." (The Ohio State University Archives.)

**A Nonfootball Rivalry, 1912.** East Oakland Avenue was a street of new homes and a little newspaper (the *Oakwood Avenue News*) that started the rivalry with the neighbor street—East Northwood Avenue. City officials of the Flower and Garden competition sponsored flower contests for the coming centennial. First prize in the city ($15) went to Oakland Avenue; second prize ($10) to Northwood Avenue. Oakland neighbors credited their victory to mass plantings of salvia, a "tax" of $1.50 per house for seeds, and the good behavior of 75–100 children on the street. (The Marshall family.)

**Gossiping About the Neighbors?** The friendly garden rivalry between Oakland and Northwood Avenues did not end with Columbus's centennial year. Neighbors on both streets took enormous pride in manicured backyard gardens. The two streets, now Northwood Historic District, were named for North Wood, a large tract of land with a mansion built by Samuel Medary, well-known Southern-sympathizer journalist. (The Marshall family.)

**AN EDUCATIONAL EXPERIMENT.** Indianola School on Sixteenth Avenue was designed by David Reibel (1907), also a university architect, for grades one through eight. However, by 1909, the school added grade nine. Columbus Schools' superintendent Shawan and Ohio State president William Oxley Thompson collaborated to redesign Indianola's curriculum to combat the high student dropout rate after eighth grade, creating the first junior high in the nation. Because of the close proximity of the school to the university, college life and neighborhood concerns were always interwoven. At the lobbying of community residents, the school became the first alternative school in the Columbus district, known for its successful "informal" elementary curriculum in the 1970s. (Doreen N. Uhas Sauer.)

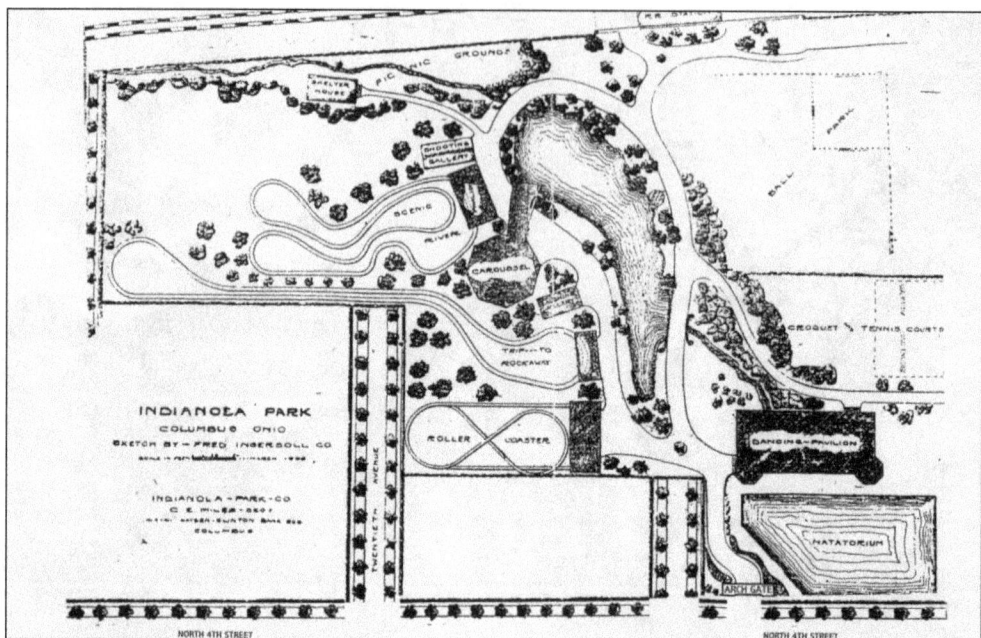

**WORLD'S LARGEST SWIMMING POOL.** Indianola Park opened at North Fourth and Nineteenth Avenues in 1904, the brainchild of real estate man Charles Miles, with a swimming pool 140 by 238 feet. Miles was a hustler. When the North Fourth streetcar line ended short of the park, Miles gathered equipment and crew on Saturday and extended the car line by Monday. Indianola Park also had the Blue Streak, one and a half miles of roller coaster on four tiers. (Doreen N. Uhas Sauer.)

**A KID'S DELIGHT.** Four artesian wells fed the pool, drawing in 30,000 gallons of water each hour through compressed air. Swimming instructors were employed each season, yet many women around 1904 were too modest to enter the pool. A covered canopy from the bathhouse to the pool allowed women to enter the water discreetly. On hot days, the pool was cooled by floating ice. On the left, the arched park entrance is on Nineteenth Avenue. (Doreen N. Uhas Sauer.)

48

SHOOT THE CHUTES. Water rides were a favorite attraction at Indianola Park, along with a working model of the Panama Canal. Vaudeville acts, a flea circus, and dance bands brought new crowds to the pavilion. The pavilion closed in 1937; the pool lasted until World War II (and is under the parking lot along North Fourth Avenue). The pavilion became an Albers Grocery store and later a thrift store. Today the pavilion has been refurbished by the Xenos Church. (Doreen N. Uhas Sauer.)

A QUIET PICNIC AREA. Much of the park's land was sold to the Columbus School Board in the late 1920s to build Indianola Junior High (1929). During construction, Native American artifacts and funeral relics were found. The former park's picnic grounds and small wooded ravine, bordered on the east side by the Big Four Railroad tracks, remain today as part of the school's extraordinarily large 11 acre playground. (Doreen N. Uhas Sauer.)

SWEETHEART OF THE AMERICAN EXPEDITIONARY FORCES. Elsie (Bierbower) Janis (1889–1956) was Columbus's hometown megastar. Dancer, singer, vaudevillian, she gave away doughnuts to doughboys on the front and, back home, outsold Harry Houdini in war bonds. Born at 337 West Fifth Avenue, she lived in the university neighborhoods, but admitted that her parents moved a great deal, seven times in one year. (Circulating Visuals, Columbus Metropolitan Library.)

CARTWHEELS ON THE LAWN. Despite her worldwide travels, Elsie's home, El-Jan, was on North High near Eighteenth Avenue (present site of a Wendy's restaurant). The large houses behind hers, barely visible, are still there. She was internationally known, and her arrival back in Columbus was newsworthy. If people gathered on the front walk, she was apt to come out to dance on the porch or do cartwheels on the lawn for their amusement. (Stuart J. Koblentz.)

THE 1913 FLOOD. West Woodruff Avenue near High Street was a residential neighborhood with large homes. Close to the river, it was a dangerous flood plain. In the 1913 flood, which devastated Columbus's west side, the Olentangy River took its toll on the modest neighborhood. Flooding (and the neighborhood) ended when the river was moved to accommodate the building of Ohio Stadium in the 1920s. (The Ohio State University Archives.)

THE
NEWEST
AND BEST
OPPORTUNITY ON THE
REAL ESTATE HORIZON

NORTH HIGH ST.

The Best is None Too Good For Your Home

## Indianola Reserve

NOW ON SALE          COME OUT TODAY

This magnificent hill has been held in reserve for thirty years. It has a commanding view, and overlooks the whole of INDIANOLA FOREST and the UNIVERSITY CAMPUS. Located at the head of IUKA and WALDECK AVES. Eastern front on INDIANOLA AVE.

LARGE AND ODD SHAPED LOTS JUST THE THING FOR THAT BUNGALOW PLAN, YOU HAVE BEEN WORKING ON. TERMS WILL BE MADE TO SUIT CUSTOMER.

### KING THOMPSON & CHAS. F. JOHNSON
915.–916 COLUMBUS SAVINGS AND TRUST BUILDING    CITZ. PHONE 2460.

THAT ODD-SIZED LOT, JUST THE THING FOR THAT BUNGALOW. King Thompson, developer of Upper Arlington, sold plats from William Neil's woods around 1913 for homes in a natural setting. Iuka Avenue was Columbus's first street to break the grid plan. Indianola Forest and Iuka Historic Districts, known for outstanding arts and crafts homes, some designed by famed architects like Frank Packard (2112 Iuka Avenue) and Charles Inscho (2058 Indianola Avenue), were in the Indianola Reserve. (Doreen N. Uhas Sauer.)

HISTORIC BRIDGE, C. 1910. Indianola bridge, like the Summit Avenue bridge, carried traffic over the Iuka Ravine and enabled the area to be developed for both residential and fraternity living. By 1912, the Chi Phis had moved from a home on Highland Avenue to 2000 Indianola Avenue (on right). The current bridge, built in the 1980s, is almost an exact replica and part of the Iuka Historic District. (Circulating Visuals, Columbus Metropolitan Library.)

**DEVELOPER HONORED IN CARTOON PORTRAIT, 1912.** The Columbus Real Estate and Improvement Company, under the direction of E. W. Crayton, featured in a Billy Ireland drawing, developed the residential Parkview, Cliffside, Glen Echo, Glenmawr Avenues, and Summit Street, adjacent to the Glen Echo Park. Arts and crafts bungalows, revival-style Tudors, and even a 1933 art deco house perch over the city-owned ravine park. Glen Echo is on the National Register of Historic Places. (Doreen N. Uhas Sauer.)

E. W. CRAYTON
President The Columbus Real Estate and Improvement Company

**JEFFREY'S HOME OWNERSHIP PLAN.** Mr. McKinley wrote about his new home on Glen Echo for the Jeffrey Manufacturing (and Mining) Company newspaper in 1920. He included this picture to promote the work of Jeffrey's Building and Loan Department, which vigorously pushed ownership for all employees. Buying a home this way was cheaper and considered a patriotic investment in America. By 1920, 134 homes had been purchased by employees in the university neighborhoods, more than were purchased in any other area. (Doreen N. Uhas Sauer.)

**HOMES WITH HORSES.** On High Street, between West Northwood and Oakland Avenues, home ownership in 1902 came with horses. C. W. Pavey needed large barns for his Friday and Saturday auctions, selling 500 horses a week or even 1,000 a day. During World War I, he moved to the fairgrounds, once selling 180 horses individually in three hours. A pre–Civil War farmhouse is just barely visible to the left. (Dr. Charles Pavey and family.)

BELL, NORTH 1996
CITIZENS 14638

# C. W. PAVEY

A MULE, A PAIR OR
A CARLOAD

## ALL KINDS OF HORSES

COLUMBUS, OHIO

"PAVEY THE MULE MAN"
2259 N. HIGH

**THE MULE MAN.** C. W. Pavey's business was helped by the work of his three sons, Hugh, Roy, and Charles, who delivered strings of 6 to 20 horses to nearby towns. Dr. Charles Pavey Jr., born in the old Pavey house, lived his entire life where he was born, went to Northwood School, old North High on Fourth Avenue, and Ohio State, completing medical schooling in 1928. Over the years, he refurbished the entire block of homes and, on some occasions, left his Rolls Royce in the driveway where he had once led horses. (Dr. Charles Pavey and family.)

**SURVEYING THE NEIGHBORHOOD.** Young Charles Pavey Jr. (on the right) takes playmates for a ride. Charles Jr. had his own Tom Thumb horse and carriage. This *c.* 1910 photograph seems to be taken in front of houses on Ramlow block where C. W. Pavey had additional horse barns. The Ramlow houses, distinctively set close together and with no setback, are said to have been motormen's houses, dating from the late 1890s. (Dr. Charles Pavey and family.)

**NEIGHBORHOOD OF STATELY HOMES.** East Lane Avenue's oldest house (still standing) dates from the 1850s, but most of the foursquare houses were built in the early 20th century. Families used deep lots to raise chickens. The horse is in a lot where 190 East Land Avenue now stands. Despite some developers' efforts to tear down, neighbors helped change zoning codes in the 1980s and most of the houses in the Indianola Forest Historic District remain. (University District Organization.)

**"MAY I HELP YOU."** Hennick's Soda Shop, originally at 1904 North High Street, catered to both neighborhood and student needs for snacks, smokes, and sweets. The Hennick business would later expand in a new location. For decades, the Hennick business, famous throughout the city, carried no address on its advertising, preferring to say it could be found "at the entrance" of the university. (University District Organization.)

**SPIFFY NEW LOT.** Neighborhoods to the south of Ohio State also participated in the 1911 garden competition. The southwest corner of High Street and Eleventh Avenue was recognized for the removal of trash and planting gardens in a vacant lot. The corners of Frambes Avenue and High Street and Smith Place and High Street, however, were not improved because owners would not give permission to volunteers. (Columbus Metropolitan Library, History and Biography.)

*Five*

# OPPORTUNITIES FOR ALL

The new decade of the 20th century and World War I changed many things at the university and in the neighborhoods for the next 20 years. Over one fourth of university men served in World War I. Racial tensions appeared in urban areas, less so in Columbus than in Springfield or Cincinnati. The university and neighborhoods faced extraordinary challenges—growth, economic depression, and aftershocks of a worldwide conflict.

Until the 1920s, young people from families of modest means generally did not go to college. The 1920s, it is recognized now, did not roar for everyone. There were poor young men who formed their own fraternity as a joke, others who worked in jobs as night watchmen and studied on the streetcar. A graduate of 1924 tells the story of a fraternity brother who went to dinner once a month at the home of a Columbus merchant and always found a $50 bill under the plate. How many lives in the 1970s would be shaped by student experiences of the 1920s, like Leo Yassenoff (a developer) or Johnny Jones (a journalist)? Both of them returned to live or work in the neighborhood because of their affection for the place.

One student from the 1920s remembers Herb and Hazel Hennick as the "hardest working and best-hearted proprietors of that food, hot fudge and soft drink emporium." Residents ate there too. Neighborhood residents and students associated in many of the same places; social events at the president's level often included people from the neighborhood. In the 1930s, neighborhood regulars included Milt Caniff, the cartoonist; Ruth McKenney, writer of *My Sister Eileen*; and Earl Wilson, Broadway entertainer writer. Jesse Owens, Olympic champion, would not find a place to live in the neighborhood.

There still were symbiotic relationships between the neighborhoods and the educational, industrial, and business systems that were located in the district. The newly-built Ohio Stadium, and its over 66,000 seating capacity, was a promise of sorts—the university would grow and the city would help to finance and fill those seats. Businesses like Columbus Oil Cloth, Ranco Corporation, Bettelle Memorial Institute, and well as Ohio State University provided jobs and opportunities for neighborhood residents who could walk or ride the streetcar to work. The late Mrs. Hedrick, an Indianola Avenue resident, remembered three things: there was only one campus policeman, officer North; paying $41 for a semester's fees; and Taps being played every day on the Orton Hall chimes.

**CIRCUS IN TOWN.** The family home and headquarters of the Heber Brothers Circus was at 312 Seventh Avenue and closed just as the Roaring Twenties approached. It had been active since 1895 and included aerialists, acrobats, wire performers, contortionists, Russian dancers, cowboys and Native Americans, ponies, donkeys, bears, and monkeys. The home housed three generations in 12 rooms, and a barn in the back housed the animals. (Circulating Visuals, Columbus Metropolitan Library.)

**SEGREGATED SOCIETY, C. 1920.** African American Baptist students gather in front of Orton Hall. Theaters, restaurants, and churches were de facto segregated. Students found housing in only a few of the predominately black neighborhoods in the area—Lane Avenue near the river, the Big Four Railroad tracks and Grant Avenue, and parts of West Eighth Avenue, where a decade earlier, Booker T. Washington routinely stayed with a family because no hotel would have him. (University Baptist Church.)

58

SMITH'S ROLLER RINK. Twenty-nine-year-old George W. Smith came to Columbus in 1889, opened a dance studio at Gay and High Streets, and later purchased land at Northwood Avenue and North Fourth Street. In 1903, he built the Smith's Iuka Dance Gardens and, the following year in a separate building, Smith's Roller Rink. From World War I through the 1960s, the facilities were booked for proms and outings. Smith died in 1941, but his wife continued to manage the rink, which closed in 1971; today the site is an apartment complex. (University District Organization.)

NEIGHBORHOOD BUSINESS. All university neighborhoods had small shops tucked into the residential areas. In 1924, at 2244 Neil Avenue, the recently built Miranda's Pharmacy featured ice cream and candy—all things neighborhood children would remember. Dorothy Miranda (on right), whose family lived at 130 West Northwood Avenue, poses behind the sign. Just out of sight is Teeter's Grocery. The pharmacy is now a real estate office. (Doreen N. Uhas Sauer.)

**BOY SCOUT TROOP 70.** From 1910 through the 1920s, the neighborhoods and the university were, on the surface, a close-knit community. May Day activities and Shakespeare plays from nearby schools were often held on campus at Browning Amphitheater. Boy Scout Troop 70 worked on neighborhood projects, under the direction of Ellery Grutt (second row, fourth from right), whose teaching career would span both Indianola schools and 40 years. (Doreen N. Uhas Sauer)

**CAMPFIRE GIRLS.** Young people at Indianola School participated in a multitude of mostly gender-segregated activities: the Sunshine Club (girls), the Honor Guard (boys), the Torch Club (boys), the Girl Reserves (girls), the True Blue Club (girls), Audubon-Forestry Club (boys), the Aircraft Club (boys), the Scrap Book Club (girls), the Kodak Club (boys), the Etiquette Club (girls), and the popular Wilko Campfire Girls (girls), seen here with a pretend fire. (Doreen N. Uhas Sauer.)

HIGH SCHOOL, JUNIOR HIGH, OR COLLEGE GIRLS? Throughout the university neighborhoods, as Ohio State grew, the average age of the population continued to become much younger than that of other areas of the city. By the 1960s, teenagers in the neighborhood, especially, became an invisible population, far outnumbered by university students. (University District Organization.)

GOOD NEIGHBOR CAMPAIGNS. In 1938, sororities and fraternities worked to be good neighbors to each other and to the community in general. Friendly invitations to neighbors to visit, a secret code of greetings across the streets (no simple hand wave), and community-building activities, like spring-cleaning, were encouraged by the Greeks. (The Ohio State University Archives.)

**READY TO MOVE, 1924.** The Poston moving trucks, owned by the Poston family near Dodridge Street, were a familiar and impressive sight in the neighborhoods—some of their best advertising came from showing off the sleek vehicles, whether on residential streets or in front of the university armory. (Sally Poston Bertolazzi.)

**THE SWEET-HENNICK HOUSE.** The Columbus Women's Club started in the living room of the William Sweet house, 1985 Waldeck Avenue. While the club would later move downtown to a mansion on East Town Street, William Sweet's pharmacy business, downtown on Long Street, would move uptown to North High Street and Wilcox Avenue. The house was also home to the Hennick family, whose landmark business was near campus. (Lynda Snashall Cummins.)

SKYSCRAPER IN THE NEIGHBORHOOD.
The William H. Sweet Company was
built in front of the residential Columbia
Court on High Street across from
Wilcox Avenue. Dr. Sweet moved his
company from two floors of a downtown
building to his new building in the
1920s. The six-story building was a
commanding presence. Residents may
not remember the size of the building
as much as one of the last tenants, the
Little Art Theater (first floor, right),
which showed some of Columbus's first
art films. (Lynda Snashall Cummins.)

SWEET'S TRIED-AND-TRUE HOUSEHOLD REMEDIES. The upper floors of the William H. Sweet
Company were used to manufacture household remedies. Most residents of the neighborhood
never saw what went on in the building until the building was empty in the 1970s. The building's
sixth floor, stripped of these fixtures, but open, afforded the curious a vista of the Olentangy
River, its flood plain, the university farms, and Upper Arlington. (Lynda Snashall Cummins.)

**NORTH COLUMBUS, 1920s.** Zann and Sammet Grocery (2604 North High Street), M. V. Clevenger Wallpaper (2602 North High), and L. Pfeiffer Grocery and Bakery (2600 North High) shared storefronts, as North Columbus continued to serve as a transportation node for local bus lines. Their neighbors were Seely's Variety Store, Buckholtz groceries and meats, and Dick's Hardware, and, according to neighbors, at least nine speakeasies. (University District Organization.)

**P. E. RUTHERFORD UNDERTAKING COMPANY, C. 1930.** The first Rutherford Funeral Home stands at 2383 North High Street (the former 1850s Maynard mansion). The Rutherfords, a pioneer family of North Columbus, were intermarried with the Beers. (William P. Rutherford.)

**LAST OF THE WYANDOTS, 1937.** Bill Moose was a highly respected citizen of the city. His family had resisted being displaced to Kansas in 1843. Young Bill Rutherford remembers being told to sit on the front steps of the funeral home and count the many dignitaries and callers on July 13–15, 1937. He thought it was a very important duty but realized, over time, it was most likely to keep him out of the way. (William P. Rutherford.)

**LINCO GAS STATION, 1925.** While the northwest corner of High Street and Blake Avenue is now a parking lot, it was for many years a gas station. The Linco brand was established in Illinois prior to World War I and, in the 1920s, was acquired by the Ohio Oil Company of Findlay, manufacturers of Marathon brand motor oil. By 1940, the company adopted Marathon as the name for its full line of products and its corporate identity as well. (Stuart J. Koblentz.)

**EAST WOODRUFF AVENUE AND HIGH STREET, 1926.** In the 1920s, Ohio Oil Company sent photographers into the field to documents its stations. This image from the corner of High Street at East Woodruff Avenue shows the businesses that once occupied High Street's west (campus) side. The largest building was the Townsend Block, at High Street and Joe Alley. By 1965, all buildings had been razed and replaced. (Stuart J. Koblentz.)

## WELLINGTON HALL

### A Residence for Men

One or two room apartments with the latest modern equipment including private bath with shower — twin beds — special room service. Excellent ventilation and abundance of light.

**J. W. BURGESS, Mgr.**
WA-2000

**North High St. at 16th Ave.**

**THE WELLINGTON.** Male students who had some money might rent rooms at the elegant and up-to-date Wellington Hall, built in 1916. Close to campus and across from the president's very own house, the Wellington was well positioned to appeal to the raccoon-coat gang, with two men's tailoring shops and cigar stores nearby. However, neighborhood residents not connected to the university were also drawn to the amenities of High Street near the campus. (Doreen N. Uhas Sauer.)

**JIM RHODES'S FRATERNITY, 1932.** From the 1920s through the 1940s, Ohio State and the neighborhoods converged on North High, across from the old Ohio Field. The Wellington Hall, Hill Tailoring, and the Wellington Drug Store made up Smitty's Corners, the place to be seen. Seen here from left to right are Bob Hill, Bill Carroll, Max Marshall, and a casually poised young Jim Rhodes, later Ohio governor. Young men, too poor to join a real fraternity, formed their own—SI-U—using a beer cap as a pledge pin. The Sixteenth and High Depression Days Alumni Association members later became civic leaders, congressmen, senators, governors, and an ambassador. (University District Organization.)

AN EARLY HENNICKS. Hennicks moved into its second building before World War I. In what might be the earliest photograph of the building, the exquisite detailing is apparent. The residential building to the right has already been added to but in a very substantial way with a stone front. Most amazing in the later photographs of Hennicks is how High Street changes. (The Ohio Historical Society.)

INSIDE HENNICKS. Customers who patronized Hennicks could find a wide array of food, sweets, and tobacco products. The store was also equipped with a Holcomb and Hoke popcorn machine. Holcomb and Hoke marketed the machines by pointing out that each individual piece of popped corn was "butter kist" by disks bathed in melted butter. The machine also roasted peanuts in a lower compartment. (University District Organization.)

**CALL FOR PHILLIP MORRIS.** In 1938, Phillip Morris's official bellboy mascot, John Roventini, paid a publicity visit to Hennicks. Roventini originated the role in 1933 after being asked to page a Phillip Morris in a hotel lobby where he worked. His distinctive style and voice gave him the job of playing "Johnny Phillip Morris" for 25 years. He did special appearances into his 70s and died in 1998 at the age of 88. (The Ohio Historical Society.)

**HENNICKS, 1940.** By the 1940s, Hennicks Soda Grill and Restaurant, 1824 North High Street, offered breakfast, lunch, dinner, sodas, beer, cigarettes, and reading material. Herb Hennick had also updated the outside of the building with gleaming vitreous tile. (The Ohio State University Archives.)

**AN ARCHITECT FOR OHIO STATE AND THE NEIGHBORHOODS, c. 1920s.** After winning a gold medal from the American Institute of Architects for his design of the Ohio Stadium, the largest reinforced concrete structure of its time to be built in the United States, Howard Dwight Smith designed the new Indianola Junior High on Nineteenth Avenue in 1928. He also designed Mack Hall and several Chicago-style apartment buildings in the university neighborhoods. (The Ohio State University Archives.)

**VISITING THE OHIO STADIUM, 1931.** Following the completion of Ohio Stadium in 1922, the horseshoe shaped stadium attracted visitors for its size and architecture. Columbus postcard books made it a tourist attraction. Such was the case when Miriam and Betty Koblentz of Cleveland drove to Columbus to visit their brother, Maurice Koblentz, a student at Ohio State, studying journalism. (Rhea Poulster.)

**GOLD MEDALS AND ALPHA PHI ALPHA.** Jesse Owens started Ohio State in 1933, despite warnings that it had one of the worst records on race relations in the Big Ten (refusing to allow two young black women to share campus housing with white women). He understood discrimination, lived in boardinghouses in the black neighborhoods, and ate hot dogs at the student union, the only eating establishment to serve him. Owens was a valued honorary member of the Alpha Phi Alpha fraternity (pictured here, Owens is in the first row, right). Ironically, though he was a man without a real place in the neighborhood in the 1930s; the neighborhood of West Oakland Avenue became the stand-in for Owens's east-side Cleveland neighborhood when a movie on Owens's life was filmed in the 1980s. (The Ohio State University Archives.)

**IN COSTUME, 1938.** Northwood School classmates David Weltner, dressed as a jester, and Jim Williams, as Uncle Sam, take a moment to have their Halloween costumes recorded for posterity. Life in the surrounding neighborhoods was filled with families and children. (David Weltner.)

**VISITING GRANDFATHER, 1937.** Roger Gibson and his mother visit Mrs. Gibson's father on East Fifth Avenue. Behind them is the commercial block (now home to Bristol Bar) and attached row housing. On the Summit Street corner, a shoe shine sign advertising services for 10¢ is still visible. Concrete block row housing, largely unchanged from the 1920s, still stands. (Roger Gibson and family.)

BATTELLE MEMORIAL INSTITUTE EMPLOYEES, C. 1939. In his last will and testament (1923), Gordon Battelle wanted to use the wealth of the Battelle family for creative research, a nonprofit organization for scientific research and exploration to be built on 10 acres of land on King Avenue. From here, work on projects as diverse as the Manhattan Project, xerography, golf balls with bounce, and candies that do not melt in the hand were developed. (Bill Brownson.)

RANCO CORPORATION. Ranco had started in a modest trolley carbarn on Indianola and Third Avenues around 1913 and grew into a major business on Fifth Avenue. The founder of Ranco invented an automatic circuit breaker for use in coal mines while working at the Jeffrey plant. Ranco moved to the site pictured here in 1936 on the former site of a city dump. In the 1950s, it manufactured refrigerators, automobile heaters, and automatic temperature controls. Battelle expanded to the site. (Doreen N. Uhas Sauer.)

**ANOTHER FIRST.** From 1934 to 1984, Big Bear Grocery at Olentangy River and Lane Avenue served the neighborhood and ran a trolley from High Street to the store. For a time, a caged bear was kept outside (for children to nag parents to shop there). It was the first self-serve supermarket in the nation, having opened only hours ahead of another in New Jersey. Housed in a former roller rink, which had been the former Crystal Slipper nightclub, and even earlier had housed polo ponies, the store's gently sloping wooden floors meant that grocery carts, left unattended, created their own swirl of action on Saturday mornings. (Circulating Visuals, Columbus Metropolitan Library.)

**OLENTANGY PARK FOOTBRIDGE, 1935.** Olentangy Park, the popular north end amusement park built by a streetcar company in the 1890s, constructed this iron footbridge to connect Neil Avenue at North Street, across the lower Rush Run (also known as Slate Run or Glen Echo Ravine) west of High Street. With the conversion of the former park in the 1930s into Olentangy Village Apartments, the bridge was torn down for scrap iron. (The Columbus Historical Society.)

## Six

# THE LONG WALK

From the 1940s through 1950s, both the physical appearance of the neighborhoods and the nature of the university and its students would change dramatically. In the 1940s, 17 fraternities closed, and their houses were taken over by the U.S. Army and Navy for trainees. With every inch of the neighborhood and the campus overflowing with returning GIs and their families, the green of the oval was preserved (there was serious talk of temporary housing). However, the neighborhoods suffered from changes in the zoning codes and lax code enforcement. Columbus billboards citywide asked citizens to open their heart and home with a vacant room. Citywide many responded, but a change in zoning laws which permitted rooming houses and high-density living. A 1954 zoning code revision happened with no notice to the community with detrimental and irreversible effects.

However, students were not the same. When the conservative university trustees imposed a gag rule against political speakers on campus, aimed at limiting liberal politics, these more-seasoned students did not want paternal oversight. They hired a sound truck and several thousand heard Paul Robeson, singer and Communist sympathizer. By the 1950s, university officials were openly calling out faculty who lived in the neighborhoods, accusing them of being Communists. A neighborhood resident's wife, who worked in the Romance Language Department, made front-page headlines as a declared Marxist. The Ohio General Assembly, like other states, had McCarthy-like hearings.

However, when there were protests, as there were in 1954 when students marched downtown to protest that they were not getting days off school to be able to attend the Rose Bowl, these seemed to be acceptable because they were on safe topics—even though thousands were involved. "The long walk" referred to the path across the oval in front of the Main Library that led directly to the university's entrance on North High Street and into the community. The university, and the neighborhoods, were poised for change.

**A GATEWAY.** Marked boundaries are symbolic. For years, the front door of the university at Fifteenth Avenue was acknowledged but not marked; students and the community moved freely through (except on game days). The university gates were phased in over time, gifts from graduating classes. The president's house, behind the marker, was the 1856 Joseph Strickler house, which predated the university but housed five presidents, the last in 1938. The house was replaced by Mershon Auditorium, and later the front door of Ohio State became symbolic with the creation of a mall. (The Ohio State University Archives.)

**OFFICER IN TRAINING, 1940.** Holding a poster for an upcoming dance, the ROTC cadet on the horse tries to persuade young women to respond to his cause for the coming event. Although armed service enrollment would begin to skyrocket just months later, April 1940 was still a time for social events. (The Ohio State University Archives.)

LONG'S BOOKSTORE, 1946. In the 1940s, Long's Bookstore, started in 1902, was the world's largest bookstore, doing $1,000 per week in retailers' orders from across the country (and the world). Col. F. C. Long and his son, R. G. Long, and 40 other employees worked in the store. By 1940, more than 1,000 Ohio State students had found part-time employment. Note the original Long's house still attached to the back of the building. (The Ohio State University Archives.)

TEMPORARY HOUSING. Taken from the top of the Ohio State University Main Library, around 1945, this image shows Ohio State's efforts to house returning students after World War II. In addition to these large white structures, other GI housing was in converted poultry barns west of the river. Despite Ohio State's efforts, neighborhoods were severely impacted when new zoning went into effect that allowed for converted multifamily dwellings and a plethora of rooming houses. (The Ohio State University Archives.)

**FIELD HOCKEY GIRLS.** The changing face of High Street can be seen in the background. Remaining residential structures were disappearing to be replaced by newly constructed businesses, especially those appealing to students. To the far right, University Theater is being built. To the left, the apartment building already houses Larry's Bar. The collection of one-story buildings in the center (where Wendy's Restaurant now stands) has a variety of businesses including a laundry and a lot for selling trailers to married students during post World War II housing shortages. This jumble of small buildings replaced El-Jan, the former home of Elsie Janis. (University District Organization.)

**DOING THE LAUNDRY, C. 1945.**
Returning students on the GI
Bill were hard pressed to find
adequate housing. A trailer
park neighborhood opened off
Seventeenth Avenue at the edge
of the fairgrounds. The trailers,
some only 14 feet long, still
provided housing for students
until the 1970s. (The Ohio State
University Archives.)

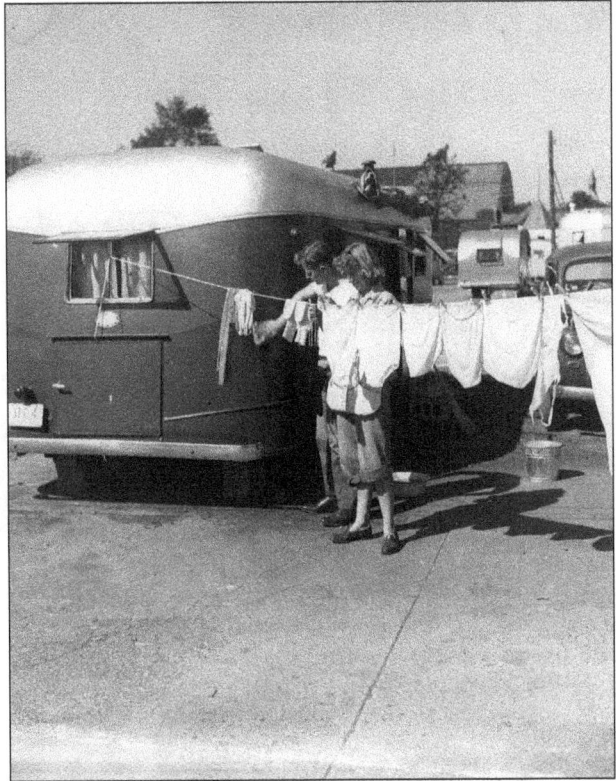

THE OHIO STATE UNIVERSITY'S

# TWILIGHT SCHOOL

WINTER QUARTER, 1947 ... *Evening and Saturday Morning Classes*

FOR ...

Army and Navy Personnel
Government Employees
Homemakers
Industrial Workers
Office Personnel
Professional Men and Women
Recent High School Graduates
Teachers and School Administrators
Veterans with Jobs and
Others Employed in Daytime Hours

100 FULL-CREDIT UNIVERSITY COURSES STARTING JANUARY 3

*For Bulletin or other information, telephone, write, or visit*

The Twilight School of The Ohio State University
UN-3148—Station 317    Columbus 10, Ohio    102 Administration Building

PLEASE POST ON BULLETIN BOARD OR PASS ON TO A FRIEND

**TWILIGHT SCHOOL, 1947.** Ohio State
adjusted to accommodate not only
returning soldiers but 1,600 Columbus
residents of all ages who attended
at night. They earned no credit and
received no grades but seldom missed
classes. For instance, a stonemason and
veteran of four armies took five classes
a week, and an elderly Woodruff
Avenue woman took psychology,
Eastern history, and philosophy to
keep up with her grandson enrolled at
Ohio State. (Doreen N. Uhas Sauer.)

79

BACK THE BOYS WITH BONDS, 1941. When the carbarns on Chittenden Avenue and High Street burned in the 1890s, the replacement streetcar barns were located north of the university at the corner of Arcadia Avenue and High Street. As the boys were returning home from war, the streetcars were in the process of leaving. General Motors Corporation had been given permission by the federal government to buy up urban trolleys and streetcars in order to facilitate automobile production and sales. (Jim and Katie Spencer.)

HIGH STREET TROLLEY LINES. Since the neighborhoods of the university formed, in large part, because of the streetcar and trolley lines, an era was ending when they were pulled up from High Street. A new era would begin in which housing development would be ruled by zoning regulations, linking uses with parking places. (The Ohio State University Archives.)

**HUDSON STREET UNDERPASS.** As automobiles took the place of streetcars, the heavy volume of traffic in and out of the neighborhoods increased to the point where it was necessary, especially in the north, to develop underpasses for traffic, like this one under the Big Four Railroad, dedicated by Gov. Michael DeSalle and Mayor M. E. Sensenbrenner in 1958. (Circulating Visuals, Columbus Metropolitan Library.)

*Congratulations*

*from*

# THE D. L. AULD CO.

**D. L. AULD.** A major employer in the Weinland Park area was D. L. Auld Company, which had been in the neighborhood since 1920. It doubled its productive capacity in a change from the manufacture of jewelry to automobile and appliance nameplates. Close to railroads and in a city with a high percentage of native-born laborers, black and white, the Auld Company attracted men and women to the area with good wages. Another large employer was Columbus Oil Cloth (later Columbus Coated Fabrics, Borden Industries) near Sixth Avenue and the Big Four Railroad tracks. (Doreen N. Uhas Sauer.)

**METHODISTS TO UNITARIANS, 1945.** The First Unitarian Church of Columbus moved from Indianola Avenue into this large former residence, formerly used by the Methodists, at 175 West Eleventh Avenue in 1945. The house met the needs of the growing organization. Later the property was sold to Ohio State University, which razed the building and replaced it with the Jesse Owens Recreation Center. (First Unitarian-Universalist Church.)

**THE SANCTIFIED GARAGE.** The growth of the Unitarian Church necessitated an addition, called "the sanctified garage" by its members. Here Rod Serling, producer of television's *Twilight Zone*, was married to the granddaughter of Ohio State University president William Oxley Thompson. (First Unitarian-Universalist Church.)

**THE ADVERTISEMENT SAYS IT ALL.** Changes in the city's zoning codes from the 1950s through the 1970s created opportunities for housing development but very little regulation in all the neighborhoods around the university. No other part of the city was affected by the AR-4 zoning. Prof. Dick Erickson, who lived on Indianola Avenue, and Les Reynolds, who lived on West Patterson Avenue, had been active in forming the University Community Association, which called for an end to overdevelopment. Although the 1970s saw much unrest for a variety of causes, the five sticks of dynamite found attached to Erickson's car in 1971 were tied to his views on stopping destruction of the neighborhoods. He received death threats, but there were no arrests. Property, as in the advertisement, was marketed for maximum use. Spurred on by these happenings, the University Community Association and the University District Organization helped downzone most of the neighborhoods and advocate for establishing the first city area commission, the University Area Commission, by the early 1970s. (Doreen N. Uhas Sauer.)

**HILLEL, 1949.** The B'nai B'rith Hillel Foundation served 800 students and 300 servicemen and their religious, cultural, and social needs at Sixteenth Avenue and Pearl Street. Hillel was perhaps best known over the years for outstanding dramas from the Hillel Players and, at this time, work on behalf of war victims in Europe. (The Ohio State University Archives.)

**HIGH STREET, 1959.** Smith's Drug Store is still there and the Wellington Hotel (no longer Wellington Hall), but a Laundromat and an independent bookstore are new. Visible to the left are the one-story retail buildouts, which attached to the houses behind them. The most nostalgic part of the image is the parking that still exists on High Street. (The Ohio State University Archives.)

84

AIR-CONDITIONED TELEVISION. James L. Snider stands in front of the Tip Tap Bar and Grill at 2404 North High Street. Snider bought the establishment in the early 1950s and he and his wife Marian operated the Tip Tap for about 10 years. The neighborhood joke was that people came in to see an air-conditioned television not drink beer. The Tip Tap was one of many taverns throughout the neighborhoods that served more residents than students—BJ's Tavern, Walt's, the Ranch, to name a few others—while others such as the Blue Danube, Ledo's, and Oldfield's appealed to both. (Marty Davis Cotrill.)

CORKY ON THE SIGNPOST. This block of buildings on the south side of High Street near Maynard Avenue is now gone. Vi Stember Flowers moved a few blocks further north to Dodridge Avenue. Henry Yee's Laundry was a neighborhood landmark. Three other Chinese families had laundries on High Street. No one knows who the child is or why he is on the pole, only that his name is Corky. (Marty Davis Cotrill.)

**WESLEY FOUNDATION STUDENTS.** Originally organized as outreach for Methodist students attending Ohio State, the Wesley Foundation, seen here at the Indianola Student Center, merged in the 1970s with the Indianola Methodist Church and the Summit Methodist Church to form the Summit Church, inclusive of all community (nearby and suburban) and student populations. See page 25 to see the house in its original setting. (Doreen N. Uhas Sauer.)

**HOLY NAME SCHOOL.** Three youngsters (from left to right, Pat Krespach, Linda Krespach, and Marty Davis) stand on the snow-covered playground of the old Holy Name School. Holy Name Parish was established in 1905, and the present church was dedicated in 1927. The school was eventually torn down to be replaced with a one-floor school (1954), which is now the Santa Cruz Church. (Marty Davis Cottrill.)

**SIXTH AND SIXTH, 1950S.** Before there was a New Indianola Historic District or a Weinland Park, the Sixth and Sixth neighborhood ruled. The playground teacher, Viola Lynch (second row, right), supervised pageants and organized the city's championship baseball team (pictured). Her husband, Dick Lynch, was a *Dispatch* reporter. Viola's out-of-state credentials unfortunately were not recognized. (Joyce Hughes.)

**WEINLAND PARK, FIRST GRADUATING CLASS.** In the 1950s, Weinland Park School graduated its first class. Built on city park property, which had been named for an activist member of city council, the class shows a large and racially diverse student body. However, no black families lived east of North Fourth Street until the 1970s. Barbara Ann Cochran (third row, right) and Joyce Hughes (first row, seventh from right) continue to live in the neighborhood. Wil Haygood, writer for the *Boston Globe*, and Curt Moody, local architect, both attended this school. (Joyce Hughes.)

**PATRIOTISM.** Boy Scouts from the Indianola Church of Christ stand at attention on Indianola Avenue, oblivious of traffic. The brick street appears to be even narrower than it is today. (Roger Gibson and family.)

**UNIVERSITY SCHOOL FAIR IN THE NEIGHBORHOOD, 1950S.** University School on campus opened in October 1932, as a laboratory and demonstration school in progressive education under Ohio State's College of Education. It started in 1930 in a home on West Frambes Avenue and continued into the late 1960s (Ramseyer Hall). The selection process gave priority to members of the faculty and siblings who already attended the school. Along with a rigorous curriculum, the school advocated self-discipline, taught sex education at all levels, and gave no grades. (University District Organization.)

**AERIAL VIEW, 1952.** From this aerial view of North Columbus, facing west, the second White Castle (1951) stands out at Arcadia Avenue and North High Street. The white porcelain coated steel building replaced the earlier white brick one. To the left of the White Castle is the used car lot for Medick Ford, which had previously been the streetcar turnaround. The largest building in the foreground is a streetcar storage barn. Glen Echo Ravine (Slate Run) appears as on open gash on the right of the image. The stream still flowed at the east side of North High Street, especially in spring. To the left of the image, two tall 19th-century buildings face each other at Dodridge Avenue and North High Street: the Ramlow Block on the north and the Nigh Brothers Grocery on the South. (The Columbus Dispatch.)

**BUILDING ST. JOHN'S ARENA.** Expansion of Lane Avenue, a new underpass west of Lane Avenue, and the building of St. John's Arena and Chemical Abstracts brought more pressure to the neighborhoods and remaining Lane Avenue housing north of Ohio State. In the distance, University Village is being built. Big Bear Grocery will remain the only constant for another decade. (The Ohio State University Archives.)

**OHIO STATER INN.** Built by developer and Ohio State enthusiast Leo Yassenoff, Ohio Stater Inn was decorated on the outside with medallions representing the university's many colleges. The Pavilion Restaurant was famous for its Pink Squirrel and Grasshopper pies, and the bar was famous as the watering hole for Ohio State's Department of English when they tired of Larry's Bar. The hotel was remodeled for student housing and a small underground shopping area. (Doreen N. Uhas Sauer.)

# Seven

# REVOLUTIONS
# AND RESOLUTIONS

Two decades of difficult times, from the 1960s through the 1970s, were ahead. In 1963, students sued the president of the university and the board of trustees, alleging deprivation of free speech. On a similar issue, the legislature introduced a bill to expand the power to ban more speakers. In 1965, students protested but this time they went inside the administration building for an all-night sit-in. Over 4,200 students signed an 80 foot petition, and by April, their demands were met.

The neighborhoods were also planning to fight when they found out that $48,500 was being given to the university to raze all residential buildings from Woodruff Avenue to Lane Avenue in order to build dormitories. Federal money from urban renewal was coming to Columbus to tear down parts of the city which were slums or had outdoor privies. However, homes north of Ohio State were clearly not slums but well-maintained residential streets. It was not just Ohio State University; the city stood to make $720,000 on the project, Battelle had plans to attract research-oriented industries to build an industrial park over the residential areas.

In 1967, a protest at Larry's Bar lasted almost six hours and involved 75 picketers when owner Lawrence Paoletti posted a sign listing undesirables who were not allowed in the bar.

In the 1970s, residents of the South Campus Association were battling with city and federal officials over the Homestead Project, which they felt would give the city money for tearing down houses. The president of the University Community Association had dynamite put under his car, presumably from developers who stood to lose if they could no longer over develop the neighborhood. North of the university, homeowners tried to stop the university's expansion through injunctions and court orders. A serial arsonist had set 100 blazes in the area.

With the May 4, 1970, Kent State University shootings, anti-Vietnam War sentiments escalated to college campuses which already were experiencing teach-ins and demonstrations. Ohio State University shut down classes and tear gas filled the neighborhoods. Only by the end of the decade and into the 1980s was there the beginning of resolution to these issues.

**REMNANTS OF HIGH STREET AND NINTH AVENUE.** The Furniture House (1500 North High Street) was operated from 1933 to 1963 by the Lucktenberg family. Bilan's Restaurant and Cocktail Lounge (1520 North High), was formerly the Hatrack restaurant. Demolished in 1963, both homes dated from 1875, built by the Kaiser brothers when cattle were still herded on High Street. At 1520 North High, Kaiser Grocery men enjoyed "coon hunting and skinning polecats out back." (University District Organization.)

**LONG'S BOOKSTORE.** Even by the 1960s, Long's Bookstore seemed to change only the billboards on top of it. The Long's sign, not visible here, had been fabricated at the Columbus Sign Company in 1948. The old Long's house, where Dr. Frank Long had been born, is still visible as an attached house. (The Ohio State University Archives.)

FIRES DESTROYS LANDMARK CHURCH, 1964. The Tenth Avenue Baptist Church was formed when members of the Russell Street Baptist Church recognized that there were no churches serving residents and students near Ohio State in 1889. Built at Tenth and Highland Avenues, the doors opened in 1890. Active work with foreign missions and Ohio State students fueled growth. The pipe organ was used by the Ohio State University Department of Music from 1913 until Mershon Auditorium was built. (University Baptist Church.)

FORWARD THINKING. Instead of using insurance money to rebuild in the suburbs, the congregation of Tenth Avenue Baptist Church purchased 12 lots on Lane Avenue, across from Ohio State, for a new church. The University Baptist Church had an enormous sanctuary, classrooms, kitchen, and dining hall to accommodate fellowship activities. Much of the success of the church was due to Dr. Carl H. Brown, who assumed the pastorate in 1962. (Joe Motil.)

THE LOST NEIGHBORHOOD. Mary Riley and her son, Jonathan, and the dog have a quiet moment on the corner of their streets, Peasley Avenue and West Woodruff Avenue. In less than a decade, the neighborhood would be lost to Ohio State University after bitter court battles and eminent domain issues. The North Residential Complex took out the neighborhood to West Lane Avenue. (Bill and Mary Riley.)

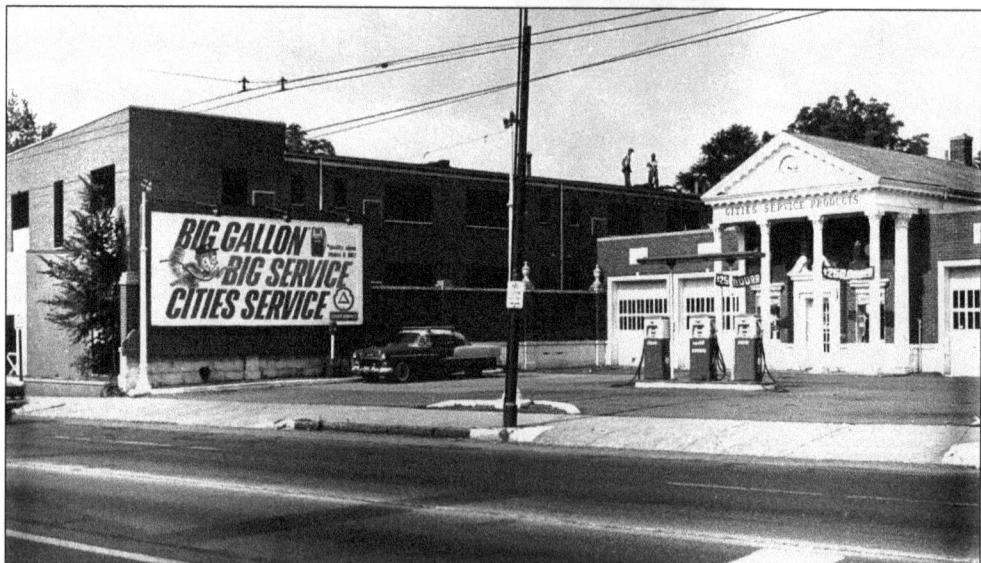

THE BEGINNING OF THE END. In 1964, this Cities Service gas station stood at the southwest corner of North High Street and West Lane Avenue. It, along with the seven-year-old Lane Terrace Apartment building to its left (under demolition) and dozens of single-family houses and businesses, was razed by 1965 to facilitate the building of Ohio State University's North Residential Complex. (The Ohio State University Archives.)

AN OCTAGON HOUSE. "Jacobs's Folly" was built in the early 1920s at 450 East Norwich Avenue by Felix Jacobs. The huge one-story house had 18-inch-thick concrete walls, a concrete roof, and a gas heating and cooling system. After spending $40,000 on a nonworking rooftop garden, Jacobs abandoned the home. In 1934, it was purchased for $4,500 and turned into apartments. It was demolished in 1974. Another apartment building stands on the site. (The Ohio Historical Society.)

THE FOLK ART MASTERPIECE. R. A. Masters worked every day for five years using only a hammer, a trowel, and a rule to create a garden of unimaginable concrete columns, pools, bridges, vases, and grottoes. Bill Arter, journalist and artist, captured only a fraction of the garden in a vignette for the newspaper. It was located at the end of West Oakland and Neil Avenues. (Bill Arter family.)

**JEAN GORDON MAKING CANDY.** Jerry Gordon and his mother, Jean, operated Gordon's Fine Candies and Ice Cream from the 1960s through the mid-1980s at 2199 North High Street. The business maintained its commercial kitchen in the old Townsend Block on the west side of High Street, south of Lane Avenue, until 1964. Jean Gordon works in the kitchen, making fondant for candy filling, while Whitney Vollmuth looks on. (Jerry Gordon.)

**GORDON'S FINE CANDIES AND ICE CREAM.** Jerry Gordon, far left, rallied the faithful for this 1969 picture outside his candy and ice-cream store, a landmark at the corner of West Norwich Avenue and North High Street. An accomplished musician, singer, and composer, Jerry Gordon used this image for the cover of his record album. (Jerry Gordon.)

**INDIANOLA JUNIOR HIGH.** By 1969, Indianola Junior High (420 East Nineteenth Avenue) had more than 1,000 students. The school was racially integrated before desegregation. December Students of the Month are, from left to right, (first row) Terri Blair, April Misiak, and Toni Neal; (second row) Rick Adkins, John Sidorenko, and Larry Davenport. The Davenport family was the first black family to live on Hamlet Avenue. Terri Blair became a Channel Six weather girl and has been married to songwriter Marvin Hamlish. (Doreen N. Uhas Sauer.)

**UNIVERSITY FLICK.** In 1965, theaters in the area included the University, later University Flick (1980 North High Street), the State Theater (1772 North High Street), the Garden Theater (1187 North High Street), the Little Art Theater (2525 North High Street), the Hudson Theater (369 East Hudson Avenue), and the old Alhambra, which later reopened as the World Theater. Many theaters closed within the next decade. University Flick now houses two restaurants. (Steve Abbott.)

**DOWN WITH JAYWALKING LAWS.** Strict enforcement of Columbus's jaywalking laws, combined with actual street arrests and bookings downtown for the infraction, pushed Ohio State University students to protest what they felt was an abuse of police authority in 1964. Stalled in the midst of the protest was the electric bus system, crippling North High Street traffic. The electric busses were soon replaced with diesel buses that could be diverted in such instances. (University District Organization.)

**ROUTINE ARREST.** A routine arrest of a youth on drug charges in 1971 erupted into tensions and eventually a riot in which 200 were arrested and 25 were injured. When the mayhem that involved up to 1,000 students was sorted out, non–Ohio State University students appeared to have started it. (Steve Abbott.)

**BORDEN BURGER.** The Borden, at 2020 North High Street, was the origin of the 1971 disturbances, although clashes between students and police happened from Tenth Avenue to Lane Avenue. A 19-year-old man was arrested by two patrolmen on a beat for ingesting hallucinogens behind the building. Within hours, clubs were swung, tear gas canisters were fired, and rocks were thrown. This Borden Burger restaurant, which stood on the site of the once bucolic El-Jan (the residence of Elsie Janis just 50 years before) closed after suffering damages in the disturbance. The site was acquired by Wendy's Old Fashioned Hamburgers, which removed the landmark big football player and successfully converted the site to one of the largest Wendy's in the history of the chain. (Steve Abbott.)

**JOHNNY JONES AND EDITH CONVERSE.** Johnny Jones, Columbus *Dispatch* columnist and Ohio State University enthusiast, was probably the most recognized man in Columbus and the least recognized in his own neighborhood on North Fourth Street, where he lived next to longtime friend Edith Converse. His "Now, Let Me Tell You" columns were popular and honest. James Thurber said, "He leaves the English language bleeding and bruised." (University District Organization.)

**EARTH SHOES.** Rick Chapman (left) and Steve Heise (right), owners of Earth Shoe store on High Street, stand on the front porch of their establishment, an old house whose front one-story addition housed Muffy McFarland's Ruby's, a popular store with one-of-a-kind baubles. Both Chapman and Heise are wearing Earth Shoes, which had "negative heels" that positioned the heel lower than the sole. (Steve Heise.)

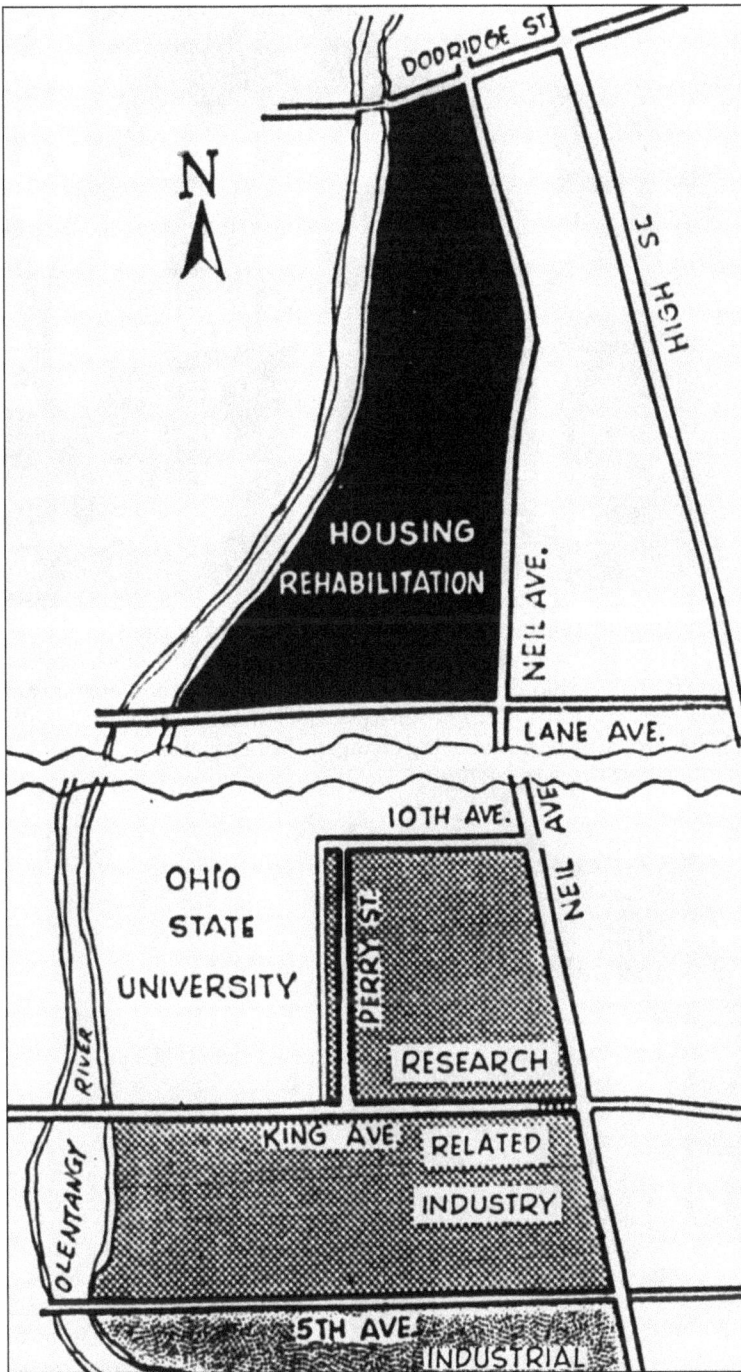

**HOLLOW PROMISE OF URBAN RENEWAL, 1963.** One of the most draconian plans to combat blight in Columbus would have bulldozed over 35 city blocks of Victorian era homes from Neil Avenue west to the Olentangy River, and from Buttles Avenue north to Tenth Avenue. Tattered Victorian grandeur would be replaced with gleaming modern research parks and industrial plants. Residents would not yield; Victorian neighborhoods were saved and improved. (Doreen N. Uhas Sauer.)

SAVING THE NEIGHBORHOOD. In the 1960s and 1970s, neighborhoods to the south of Ohio State University had been labeled as deteriorated and unsafe. Demolitions happened, and letters between the city, Battelle, Ohio State University, preservation groups, area commissions, and the neighbors flew back and forth. The University Area Commission and the University District Organization helped to bring positive zoning changes. (Bill Brownson.)

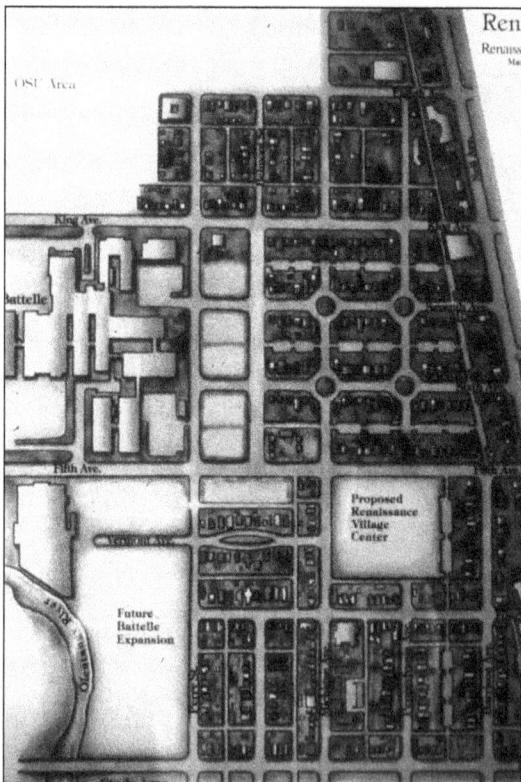

RESIDENTIAL RESTORATION. Battelle owned hundreds of properties in the neighborhoods and was ordered by the courts to divest itself of its holdings (since it was a nonprofit corporation). Forming Renaissance Realty, Battelle stabilized the houses and began to sell them. A market-based renewal program had emerged from the previous redlining of the area, as seen on page 101. (Doreen N. Uhas Sauer.)

MOBILE HOMES. Some properties that were deemed too deteriorated to be saved were demolished, and others were moved out of areas that would see new residential development. (Bill Brownson.)

HOUSES IN NEW PLACES. A small cluster of substantial homes were moved into a courtyardlike setting, which has sometimes been called the University District's version of a mobile-home park. The houses were restored in their new locations and the area received a noticeable upgrade when a former Ohio governor bought one to be his home. (Bill Brownson.)

**SWEEPING CHANGES.** Using the theme "sweeping changes," many streets and neighborhoods began regular street and alley cleanups. Longtime community activists Sharon Austin and Barbee Durham are seen here in an alley off Seventeenth Avenue. Barbee Durham was a retired Ohio State University professor and former president of the NAACP in Columbus who lived on Seventeenth Avenue; Sharon Austin lived on Nineteenth Avenue and worked at the University District Organization. (University District Organization.)

# HELP
## KEEP OUR
## ALLEY CLEAN
*Thank You*
### TUTTLE PARK NEIGHBORHOOD ASSOCIATION
### UNIVERSITY COMMUNITY ASSOCIATION

**ESTABLISHING A PRESENCE.** The Tuttle Park Neighborhood, from Neil Avenue to the Olentangy River and West Lane Avenue to Dodridge Street, was the last neighborhood to change its zoning through resident action. It joined with the larger organization, the University Community Association, to post litter signs in alleys, notifying the many visitors who came for football that this was a neighborhood. (Doreen N. Uhas Sauer.)

**THE NEIGHBORHOOD VINEYARD.** For over 80 years, the grape arbor grew next to a small floral shop at Sixteenth Avenue and High Street. A welcome patch of green on an urban street, the arbor was removed for construction in the 1980s. Residents took pieces of vine home with them to continue it. When the Wexner Center for the Arts was under construction, tendrils of the vine were seen sprouting on the other side of High Street. (University District Organization.)

**SON OF A SON OF A COBBLER.** Steve Cherkas was an expert in leather working, and he came by his trade naturally from his father and grandfather, who had been cobblers. What many customers did not know was Cherkas was also a neighborhood resident and lawyer, who preferred his lifestyle in his step-down store at the corner of East Norwich Avenue and North High Street. (Doreen N. Uhas Sauer.)

**LUNCH OUTSIDE AT FREDDIE'S.** The big hair, the sideburns, the plaids, the intensity—it must be the 1970s with medical students having lunch on Neil Avenue across from Ohio State University's Hamilton Hall. (The Ohio State University Archives.)

**A LEGEND IN ITS OWN MIND.** Papa Joe's could be rowdy. It was both a student and community gathering spot, especially before football games. It burned down before it could become part of the new South Campus Gateway project. To the left was the Richardson Romanesque Yee's Laundry building. Campus Partners, the nonprofit development corporation that oversees the gateway, agreed to number the bricks and preserve the facade for possible future use. (Dick and Sandy Allen.)

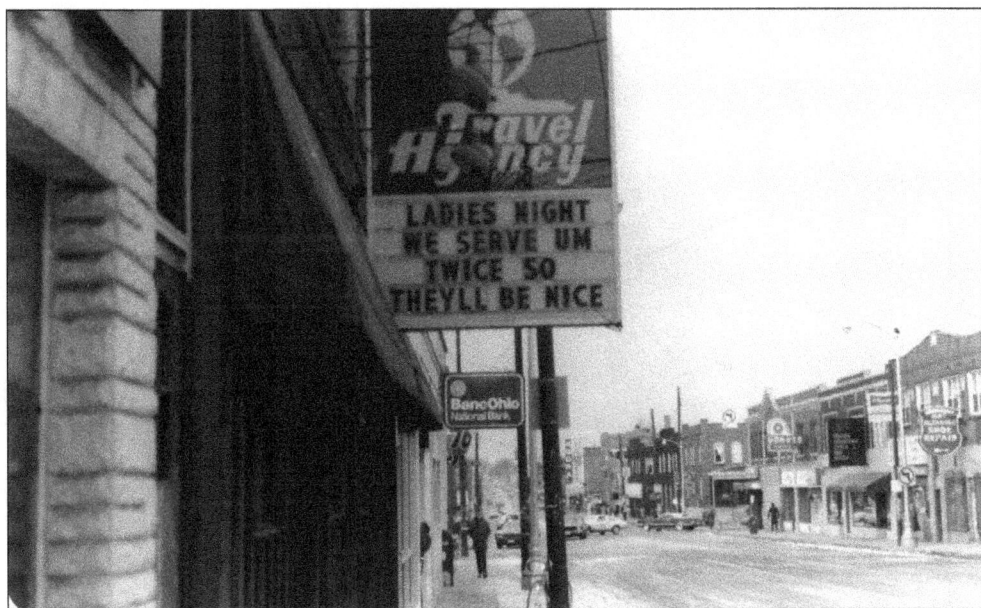

**TRAVEL AGENCY.** There is no hidden message in this sign. The Travel Agency and other bars in the district were so packed on weekends that police strung ropes from pole to pole to keep patrons from falling in the streets. All the buildings, on both sides of North High Street, up to where the cars are turning, later were demolished for the South Campus Gateway project. (Dick and Sandy Allen.)

**THE GIVERS.** Every community has them—the wise ones who pass down their knowledge to the children of the neighborhood. Ruth Schultz, even in advanced age, gathered Girl Scouts to her and taught them how to plant bulbs in Tuttle Park and in neighborhood boulevards, teaching not only horticulture but also a sense of owning the neighborhood. Dorothy Cromartie in Weinland Park organized Camp Fire Girls and community activities until she was well past age 90. (University District Organization.)

MISSING NEIGHBORHOOD LANDMARKS. The proliferation of schools in the 1900s, seven decades later, created a surplus of schools. Families who lived south of the university were hit especially hard by the disinvestment and redlining. Ninth Avenue School, built in 1896 at the corner of Ninth Avenue and Worthington Street, was demolished. Some schools survived, like (the first) Indianola School. (Jonathan Riley.)

THE AFTERMATH. In 1982, the landmark Northwood School was destroyed in a spectacular and mysterious fire. The 1905 annex remained as a recycling center. The remains of the building, as seen from the south, were a sad end to a building that helped to define the north campus neighborhoods for more than a century. The Northwood High Building now occupies the site. (Jonathan Riley.)

**BURGER KING WITH A TWIST.** What might be most interesting in this image is not a fast food restaurant but the downstairs of the building on North High Street, just north of East Lane Avenue. The Campus Underground was a short-lived basement venture (along with an electronics store and a tailor) that rented the spot after the original developer met with neighborhood resistance about putting in a topless bar. The building has been replaced by a CVS drugstore. (University District Organization.)

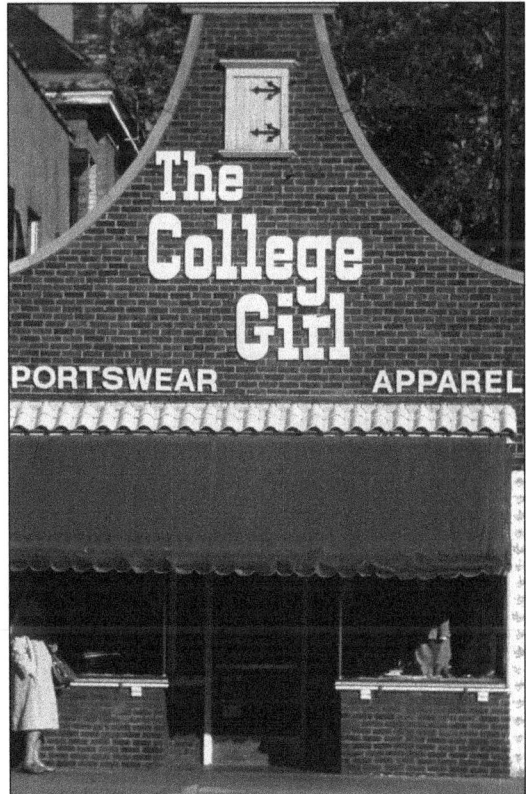

**COLLEGE GIRL.** So many women in Columbus started shopping in this store while in college and continued long after they were out of college that it was rumored it could be renamed College Matron. Like other businesses on High Street between Fifteenth and Seventeenth Avenues, the store at 1924 North High Street was a one-story addition to the front of an old house, originally built as the Marmac Tea Room, which later became the Sutch Tavern and then the Dutch Chocolate Shop (1930–1950) and had real delft tile on the facade. (University District Organization.)

**TRADE WINDS.** Libby Gregory organized the first Community Festival, spoke out on women's issues, organized Earth Day activities, and edited the *Free Press*. She owned Amorosa di Prospero and the Blue Griffin, retail shops in Pearl Alley, but her Trade Winds on High Street was the informal center of community organizing, where she put out the *Free Press* in 1972 when the staff was jailed. When Tradewinds closed, the mural was whitewashed. (University District Organization.)

12 E. 15th Avenue

1912 North High Street

BY OUR QUALITY
WE SHALL BE KNOWN

**CHARBERT'S AND CHAR BAR.** Two separate businesses, sometimes referred to by the locals as "Clean" or "Dirty" Charberts, Dirty Charberts was the preferred location for students, insomniac residents, and local color from the community at large. (Emily Foster.)

**THE VENETIAN.** Another residential house converted to a business, the Venetian Restaurant on East Frambers Avenue was popular with students and residents alike, serving a distinctive basil, thyme, and sweet-cheese pizza. The walls were adorned with hand-drawn murals depicting Venice. (University District Organization.)

**STREET SCENE AND THE AGORA.** The former State Theater, from the 1930s, with its white terra-cotta facade, has had many names and many venues—the Agora Ballroom (1970), the New Port (1983), and Newport Music Hall. Its list of stars is as long as its history. The theater bills itself as the oldest continuing rock club in the country. The Street Scene, fondly remembered for its chicken wings (before anyone else had them), was also a popular spot for engagements. (University District Organization.)

**Two White Castles.** A once-in-a-lifetime scene was the passing of an early "porcelain palace" White Castle and another of its type in the early 1980s, when the High Street and Arcadia Avenue White Castle met its Cleveland Avenue cousin on its way out to a small outdoor museum in Grove City, Ohio. (Doreen N. Uhas Sauer.)

**Tuttle Park.** Every year, a hot air balloon was used for an event at the fairgrounds and brought by the Pavey family to Tuttle Park for the neighborhood children. The park's creation was a city and university project. The city and Ohio State University helped to acquire property for Tuttle Park, named for the beloved newspaper sports editor Clyde Tuttle, or "Tut," who died in 1929. When Tuttle Park opened in 1930, it was the largest park in the city for children. In 1932, the park was a well-researched birding spot, documented by famed ornithologist Margaret Morse Nice, who lived in the neighborhood. (Cynthia Pavey Rieth.)

THE BIKE LANE. Designed to be protective and conscious of bike riders, it was the first, and last, bike lane for the city, implemented on North High Street. Riders were confused, thinking it was for both directions of traffic. The real issue, however, was keeping it clean. The city, never having a bike lane before, said the gutterlike lane was property of the parks department, who said it belonged to traffic and circulation. (The Ohio State University Archives.)

MORE ACTIVE THAN DOWNTOWN. In a view looking south from Mershon Auditorium at High Street, the variety of signs may look distracting and cluttered, but the business district was more alive than downtown Columbus. Part of the reason was the number of independent retailers that could operate best in smaller spaces and the estimated daytime population of the district of almost 100,000 people. (The Ohio State University Archives.)

113

THE CENTER OF THINGS. In an undated picture, from left to right, Dick Erickson, University Community Association; Tom Moody, mayor of Columbus; and Linda Ridihalgh, University District Organization, are pictured in a reception that inaugurates the marketing debut of the "University Community: The Center of Things" (note their buttons). The late 1970s and early 1980s marked the beginning of some positive steps and new collaborations to rebuild two decades of erosion in the neighborhoods. (University District Organization.)

THE WELCOME. An annual event for many years was being a watering station for the Columbus Marathon runners as they came through the neighborhood. The runners, who had most of the race before them, were through in minutes, but the party and gathering lasted into the afternoon. (Doreen N. Uhas Sauer.)

# *Eight*

# OUTSIDE LIES THE MAGIC

In its more than 150 years of history, from the mid-1800s through the 1970s, the neighborhoods that surround the university have acquired no small shortage of mysterious changes, vintage landmarks, legendary stories, unusual buildings, and interesting adaptive reuses. John Stilgoe, an Orchard Professor of Landscape History at Harvard University, wrote a small book titled *Outside Lies Magic: Regaining History and Awareness in Everyday Places.* In every sense of the words in that title, this last chapter is designed to arouse the curiosity of those who sometimes wonder about everyday places.

Stilgoe explores why electric lines, mailboxes, or backyards are designed the way they are. A walk in any Ohio State University neighborhood provokes the same curiosity. Why is one street a row of tiny farmhouses, located only 50 feet from rows of large brick houses? Why do most houses in the district have stained-glass or opalescent glass in side-yard windows? Shouldn't there be more decorative chimney pots on the ostentatious Victorian homes? Why are double houses side-by-side and not up and down? Why were Joe, Doe, and Moe Alleys named? What happened on that corner? Who lived here before? What streets created racial barriers? Why do some abstracts trace ownership to the Moravian missionaries for "the conversion of the heathen" and others give land to refugees from Canada? And who in heaven's name are all these streets named for?

This chapter includes only a few questions and a few answers. Readers can add their own questions, because outside lies the magic. Readers are also encouraged to contact the University District Organization with more stories, pictures, memories, and/or corrections, as another book is planned.

**THE BEFORE.** Dr. Charles Pavey Jr., who had lived his entire life on North High Street practicing medicine and raising his own children, took a life-changing trip to Williamsburg, Virginia, and came home with a plan to remodel the properties he was acquiring. (Cynthia Pavey Reith.)

**THE AFTER.** People still wonder about how these houses changed. Starting about 1950, the Pavey family lived for many months in chaos on the second floor of their own home while workman changed the American foursquare-style houses into rows of Williamsburg-looking elegant townhouses. Colonial details were incorporated—a cornice trim, a stone step, an ornamental yard decoration. (Cynthia Pavey Reith.)

**THE ELIZABETH HOME.** The large house at West Patterson and Williams Streets has mystified passersby for decades. Out of character with the rest of the residences, it is divided into many apartments. The house was the Elizabeth Home for Girls in Distress (unwed mothers) and was privately funded by a neighborhood resident. (Stuart J. Koblentz.)

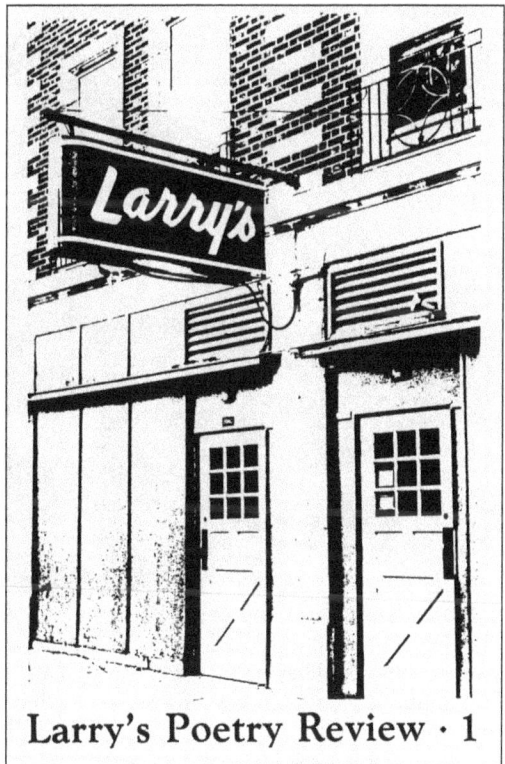

**LARRY'S POETRY REVIEW.** Larry's Bar (established in the 1920s) just ended its long run as a gathering place at 2040 North High Street. It may be hard to pass a bar and think poetry, but Larry's was the site of frequent poetry readings. This image is the cover of the first edition (1986) of *Larry's Poetry Review*, edited by Steve Abbott. Rumors about its being a gay bar were floated by the patrons to discourage undergraduates from visiting. (Doreen N. Uhas Sauer.)

**Larry's Poetry Review · 1**

**JOHN DEWEY AND THE THISTLE STOP BATHROOM.** John Dewey (1859–1952), famous progressive educator, visited Ohio State and stayed somewhere in the neighborhood. According to Ruth Shuman McLean, who owned Thistle Stop on East Frambes Avenue, John Dewey stayed there. Over the years, the story of his demand for his own private bathroom was repeated. However, it should be said Dewey was not a demanding type and bathrooms were not built overnight. Most likely, Dewey's famous bathroom was one made accessible from a bedroom. (Stuart J. Koblentz.)

**THISTLE STOP.** In 1948, Ruth Shuman McLean and Dr. Milton McLean bought 196 East Frambes Avenue and rented rooms to international students and scholars while their children attended school. They had worked throughout their lives for world peace. Dr. McLean had been president of Lincoln College and came to Ohio State as the first coordinator of religious affairs in a state university. In 2004, Dianne and Ed Efsic bought the house to continue the tradition. (Stuart J. Koblentz.)

THE HOUSE OF A HERO. Civil War Union veteran William Knauss had no reason to like Confederates, but passing the unsightly Confederate Cemetery, Camp Chase on Columbus's west side, he was horrified to think that any solider would not have an honorable resting place. He and his son-in-law began to restore Camp Chase and placed markers to honor the fallen. The first Sunday of June, Confederate Memorial Day is held there because of Knauss. (Stuart J. Koblentz.)

THE HOUSE THAT IS NOT THERE. Dennison Place is part of the Near North National Register of Historic Places district and was a first urban renewal area. It has always been filled with community activism. Residents formed a civic group in 1972, and Pete McWane and Jean Hansford published the famous *Neighborhood Busybody*. But the area also has two views on historic preservation oversight, One opinion is to do whatever the owner wants, like this artistic facade. The front of the house is quite literally not there. The bay window and trim are all artifice, fool-of-the-eye art, perfectly flat and constructed of slivers of stone and shades of paint, a creation of love. (Stuart J. Koblentz.)

ORTON LAB. This Beaux-Arts-style building sits in the middle of a modest residential area. The Orton Ceramic Foundation, founded by Edward Orton Jr., was an early think tank that experimented with new techniques and products in ceramic engineering. The father and son's work was so important that the location of the building was permitted in a residential area. They made the building as attractive as possible. (University District Organization.)

A FIRST IN OHIO. The stone chapel at Ninth and Indianola Avenues was the first Mormon house of worship built in Ohio since the Kirkland Temple in the 1830s and signified the return of the Mormons to Ohio. Dedicated in 1930, the chapel was an improvement from their rented house across the street. The chapel served the members for 30 years and is now the St. Sophia's Orthodox Church. (Stuart J. Koblentz.)

Glenn Echo Park, Columbus, Ohio

GLEN ECHO RAVINE, 1912. Glen Echo Ravine is part of a system of creeks and ravines that stretches from the Iuka Ravine to beyond Worthington, Ohio, emptying into the Olentangy River. Through the heart of Glen Echo, Slate Run passes through an 1860s stone chase, created by railroad construction, on its way to the Olentangy River. For a time, the ravine was used as a camp for patients with tuberculosis. After a proposal to relocate Protestant (now Riverside Methodist) Hospital was abandoned, developer E. W. Creighton acquired the area and developed it as the residential Indianola Park View by 1907. When development within the ravine proved too difficult to undertake, the unused land was given to the city for use as a park. Today the neighborhood, on the National Register of Historic Places, is better known as Glen Echo. The Glen Echo Ravine, still a city-owned park, has become a conservation area. (Stuart J. Koblentz.)

**TERRA-COTTA CHIC.** Charles W. "Chic" Harley, a three-time All-American (1916, 1917, 1919), drew record-breaking crowds to Ohio Field on High Street. Commercial-property developer Leo Yassenoff, a 1915 Ohio State football player, placed Harley's likeness on the facade of his new University Theater. "Terra-cotta Chic" has recently been liberated from appearing to be climbing over an awning of a restaurant and continues to play ball across from the field he made famous. (University District Organization.)

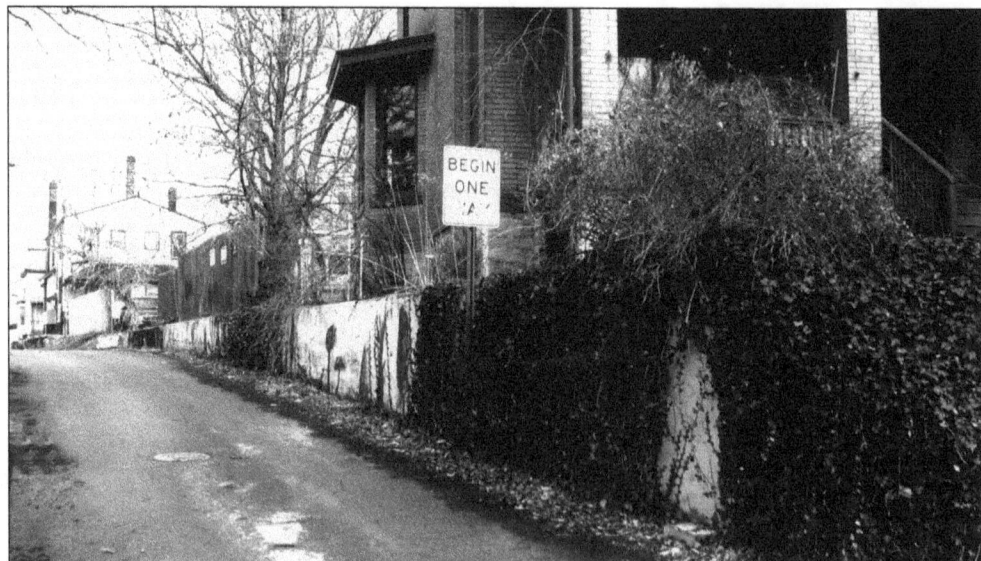

**THE WALL.** Beginning in the 1960s, this section of retaining wall on the first alley east of High Street at Oakland Avenue was known as "the Wall" by gay Ohio State students and local residents who cruised the area. The Wall had a special "no turn" sign to discourage traffic, but by the 1970s, it was no longer a discreet place for rendezvous. It is now a memory of Columbus GLBT (gay, lesbian, bisexual, transgender) history. (Stuart J. Koblentz.)

HARE ORPHANAGE. The beautiful stone building at 2104 Tuller Street was once the Hare Orphanage, which moved to this location in 1915 from a large mansion on Woodland Avenue. Joseph Hare died at 90 years old in 1859. A philanthropist, he bequeathed his fortune to orphans, but left his nine children nothing. His wife received an annuity of $500 if she remained single. Plagued by problems, the orphanage ceased to operate. (Stuart J. Koblentz.)

THE WHEELBARROW MANSION. The Felix Jacobs mansion with its three-story tower, built about 1905, is a standout in the Weinland Park neighborhood. Industrial baron Jacobs had all the showplace conveniences of the day for his home—central heating, electricity, and a telephone (not speaking tube) system. He and partner James Kilbourne founded the Kilbourne and Jacobs Manufacturing Company, whose wheelbarrow and horse-drawn earth-moving equipment was in worldwide demand. (Stuart J. Koblentz.)

**THE SINNER.** Dr. James Snook was a prominent Ohio State University professor who won a gold medal for his expert use of pistols in the 1920 Brussels Olympic Games. A quiet, well-mannered man who lived in the neighborhood and attended King Avenue Church, he was suddenly arrested after the body of Theora Hix was found in a quarry in 1929. Broadcast on radio, the trial was sensational, and Mrs. Snook sat at his side, hearing the story of infidelity, drugs, and deviant sex. James was executed in the Ohio Penitentiary in 1930, making him the only gold medal U.S. Olympian to be executed for a capital crime. (The Ohio State University Archives.)

**THE SIN.** Although Hix and Snook had a rented room at 24 Hubbard Avenue, the apartment above this building on Neil Avenue was, for a time, her apartment that she shared with a roommate. The roommate reported her missing. Snook claimed self-defense, but providing the details was no easy matter on radio or in the newspapers of the time. Underground transcript printings were published for those who wanted lurid details. (Stuart J. Koblentz.)

**THE REDEEMED.** Dr. William Oxley Thompson's tenure at Ohio State preceded the Snook crime, and Snook attended the King Avenue Methodist Church, but Dr. Thompson would not have left his sheep to stray. This stone, outdoor pulpit, constructed into the side of Indianola Presbyterian Church on Waldeck Avenue, was the special pulpit of university president Thompson. In good weather, he might choose to preach from here, and he expected a very respectful turnout of students to gather round. The church was in the heart of student housing and it would have been almost impossible to sneak away and not be noticed by Dr. Thompson. (Stuart J. Koblentz.)

MEDARY SCHOOL. At 2500 Medary Avenue, a large gabled school stands out in the neighborhood. Designed by school architect David Riebel, who was fond of dormers and Romanesque arches, the school was finished in 1892. At one time, there was a large opening between the first and second floors in the main hall, designed so that teachers and principal could have students gather around the openings on both floors and have announcements yelled to them. (Stuart J. Koblentz.)

THE OPEN AIR SCHOOL. Youngsters with tuberculosis attended the Neil Avenue School, located on the Olentangy River at Hudson Street, in order to breathe in the healthy river air around 1910. Children virtually lived at the school, studying, taking naps, eating properly, bundling up for outdoor naps, and studying again—all in small increments throughout the day. The large doors were for taking cots and bedding outside. Today the building, the Neil Avenue School, is the offices for Columbus city schools. (Stuart J. Koblentz.)

THE NEW INDIANOLA JUNIOR HIGH, 1928. Tucked behind a still-existing building from the 1904 Indianola Park, Indianola Middle School, at 420 East Nineteenth Avenue, was the first junior high in its own building (designed by Howard Dwight Smith). The outside terra-cotta details and the door surrounds were done by Dr. Erwin Frey a professor at Ohio State. The library is richly ornamented and has a working fireplace. Details, like the teachers' mailboxes, came from the original Indianola School. The school remains, essentially, a neighborhood school, drawing from nearby streets. (Doreen N. Uhas Sauer.)

CHIEF TAHGAJUTE, 1928–1980. The Mingo Indian name *Tahgajute* means "one who looks over his eyelashes"—or one who overcomes obstacles. Chief Tahgajute's image was carved in the attic of the old Indianola School on Sixteenth Avenue by Dr. Erwin Frey, Ohio State professor of fine arts. Frey created the stone relief while he was in the process of finishing the statue of university president William Oxley Thompson for the Ohio State University Main Library. Indianola students chose the historic reference which today is on the facade of Indianola Middle School. Stone animals, once native to the area, and arts and crafts tiles on the facade are also Frey's work. In the 1980s, Tahgajute was chosen again to be the symbol of the energy and imagination of the university community. (University District Organization.)

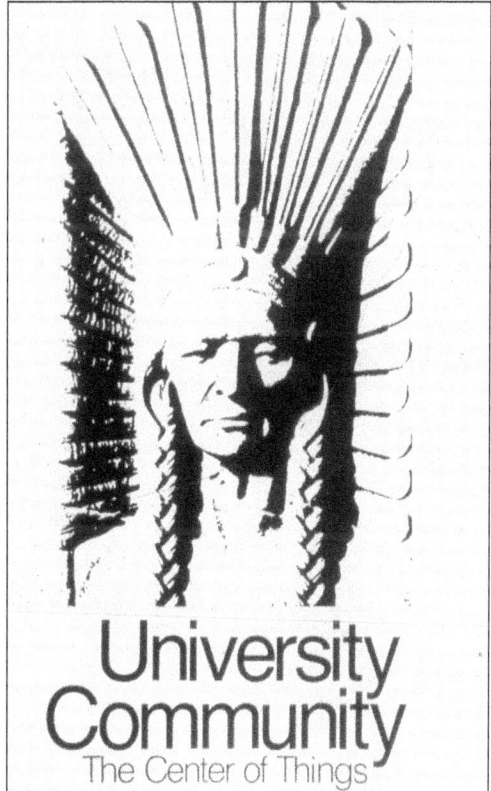

University Community
The Center of Things

Visit us at
arcadiapublishing.com

www.ingramcontent.com/pod-product-compliance
Lightning Source LLC
Chambersburg PA
CBHW050710110426
42813CB00007B/2139